CHRISTIN ROSA

SAVING NATE

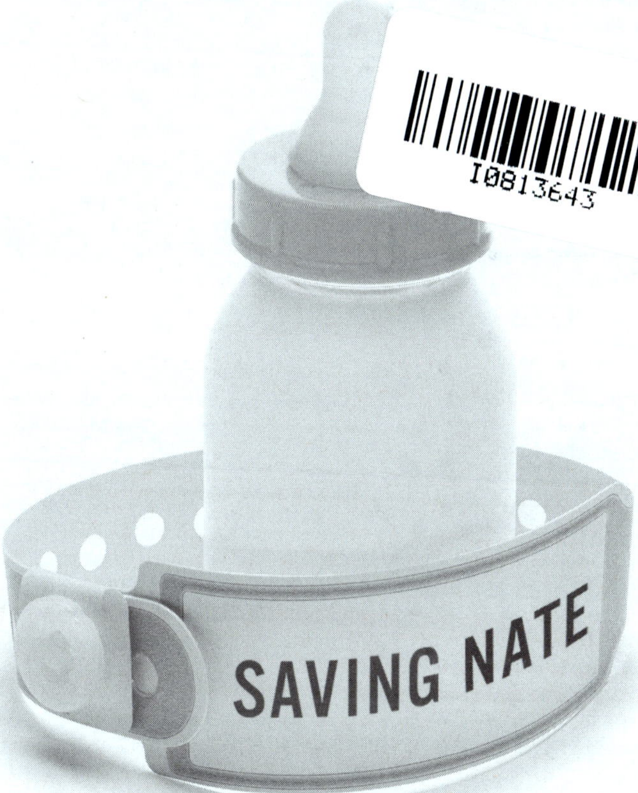

Choosing *Life* after a Devastating Prenatal Diagnosis

A Focus on the Family resource
published by Tyndale House Publishers

Saving Nate: Choosing Life after a Devastating Prenatal Diagnosis

A Focus on the Family book published by Tyndale House Publishers, Carol Stream, Illinois 60188

Cover design by Molly Van Borstel, Faceout Studio

Interior design by Cathy Miller

All stories in this book are true and are used by permission. Some names, locations, and details have been changed to protect the privacy of those involved.

For information about special discounts for bulk purchases, please contact Tyndale House Publishers at csresponse@tyndale.com, or call 1-855-277-9400.

ISBN 978-1-64607-183-8

Printed in the United States of America

32 31 30 29 28 27 26
7 6 5 4 3 2 1

Saving Nate not only reiterates the truth of the preciousness of every human life but also lays out a road map for how to persevere in faith. Christin Rosa and her husband, Mauricio, never gave up, even while being pressured by multiple doctors to abort their baby boy. Their witness is inspiring, and this book is a must-read for anyone who's ever received an unfavorable prenatal diagnosis.

> **Abby Johnson,** Planned Parenthood clinic director turned pro-life advocate; author of *Unplanned* and *What's in Mommy's Tummy?*

Saving Nate is a powerful and deeply moving testament to the unwavering love of a mother and father who chose life for their child in the face of overwhelming uncertainty. Christin Rosa's journey through a devastating prenatal diagnosis and her steadfast trust in God's plan echo the stories of many families who've been pressured to view their children's lives as disposable. As someone who lived the reality of surviving an abortion and has dedicated my life to advocating for the dignity of every human being, I am profoundly moved by the courage, faith, and resilience displayed in these pages. This book is a deeply personal reminder that every life is a gift from God.

> **Melissa Ohden,** founder and CEO of the Abortion Survivors Network and author of *Abortion Survivors Break Their Silence*

Christin's account of her pregnancy with Nate is not only engaging, suspenseful, and heartwarming but also maddening. Her faith, courage, and perseverance against all odds are inspiring. Yet her treatment by those whose job it was to care for her and her baby is shocking, especially the insensitivity and stark callousness of the doctors she encountered. For me as an obstetrician, it was enlightening to read her perspective as a patient. Are babies—especially if they're not "perfect"—considered disposable? This book is a must-read for anyone in the field of obstetrics. Attitudes must change, and I believe Christin's story will help make a difference.

Dr. Patti Giebink, retired obstetrician, former abortion doctor, and author of *Unexpected Choice: An Abortion Doctor's Journey to Pro-Life*

I've heard from many moms and dads who've been told, "Your baby is incompatible with life" or "He (or she) won't live very long." And with each story my heart breaks. That's why I'm so thankful for *Saving Nate*. Author Christin Rosa and her husband, Mauricio, don't hide the struggles they faced when they received a devasting diagnosis. They share their fears and doubts even as they know their comfort and provision comes from our Father in heaven. As Christin writes, "He's the One who holds us tightly. . . . It's to Him we must cling." And as Mauricio says, "we're people of life, so we'll always fight for life." If you or someone you know is walking this journey, this book won't change a diagnosis—but it will bring hope where there is hurt.

Robyn Chambers, vice president of advocacy for children at Focus on the Family

From the very first page, I could hear the roller coaster; I felt myself on the same ride that Christin describes. The emotions, the impossible choices—no parent should ever have to face them. I, too, was presented with the option to end my baby's life following a prenatal diagnosis, and I also made the choice to carry her to term. The courage Mauricio and Christin showed in the face of fear is extraordinary. The faith and hope they carried with them through every step of this journey is a beautiful gift to the reader. I'm deeply grateful for Christin's vulnerability in sharing her story and for the hope she offers with each word. *Saving Nate* is a sacred offering of strength and courage to everyone who reads it.

Laura Huene, BSN, RN, CPLC, founder of String of Pearls (perinatal hospice) and life coach with the Purpose Project

I worked with Mauricio Rosa when Nate was born, so reading Christin's account of their journey reminded me of the faith this couple displayed during the many highs and lows of that time. Their confidence in God was and is an inspiration to me. More importantly, this is a story of God being greater than the odds Nate faced. *Saving Nate* will encourage you to celebrate and stand for the gift of life.

Kirk Giles, copastor of Forward Church in Cambridge, Ontario, and former president of Promise Keepers Canada

The hero of *Saving Nate*, as Christin makes so clear, is our Lord, Jesus Christ. Her story is a testimony that despite a death-embracing culture, Christ is not done with Canada. *Saving Nate* will encourage you, inspire you, and embolden you to share the hope of Jesus Christ.

Matthew Harper, executive director of Speak for the Unborn

Christin writes a courageous, compassionate, and hope-filled testimony of God's goodness in the most uncertain and heartbreaking circumstances. In a world where a prenatal diagnosis is often met with fear and the pressure to choose death, this book stands as a beacon of truth, love, and unwavering faith. Page after page, it offers another way with the gentle yet firm reminder that all human life has value. *Saving Nate* is not just a book—it's an *encouragement* to trust God even when the odds seem stacked against you. Whether this could be your story or you simply want to learn more, this book will encourage you in your faith and in your resolve for life.

Jojo Ruba, founder of RedeemingConversations.ca

Honest and thought-provoking, *Saving Nate* takes the reader into the depths of the Rosa family's fight for their baby's life. Christin takes the reader on a real and raw emotional roller coaster of trusting God while standing firm against the doctors' "reduction" advice. Highly recommended.

Sandra Gullacher, operations manager for Life Room

Reading *Saving Nate* felt like I was not only watching the events of Christin Rosa's life unfold—I could also imagine the emotional ups and downs she and her husband faced. I felt myself cheering them on! Under pressure from medical professionals to abort Nate, Christin and Mauricio did not consider abortion to be an option as their relationship with Jesus guided them and they leaned on Him. This is an essential book for anyone who is considering abortion because their unborn child has some abnormalities or might not survive. Well done, Christin. Thank you for letting us journey with you and for inspiring us!

Greg Musselman, minister-at-large with the Voice of the Martyrs Canada and former host of *100 Huntley Street*

As someone who has experienced the devastating trauma of a past abortion, I can personally attest that abortion is never the answer it's presented to be. *Saving Nate* is a poignant and beautifully written page-turner that sheds light on realities many parents face yet are rarely talked about. Christin offers hope and encouragement, even when everyone around her seems to be pushing for death. She compassionately unpacks situations that others might face and highlights the importance of knowing God and His Word. Her story is informative, educational, and deeply moving. My prayer is that this book will change many hearts and minds about the value of life and ultimately direct readers to our Lord and Savior, Jesus Christ.

Jocelynn Rodrigues, founder of Restored and Redeemed Ministries and speaker for RedeemingConversations.ca

It was difficult for my tear-filled eyes to focus on Christin Rosa's account of the battle for her son Nathaniel's life, yet it was even harder to put down the book, because my emotional state kept me glued to each page. Christin presents a beautiful, heart-wrenching tale that artfully weaves her background and marriage to Mauricio with the struggles the couple faced when they discovered she was pregnant with twins. The voices around them shouting death were loud, but more powerful was their trust in Jesus Christ.

Marie-Blanche Mitchell, retired teacher and author of *Loving Zoe*

Saving Nate is a profoundly beautiful journey of faith, medicine, and God's grace cooperating in our world. We witness a family trust in God's divine plan regardless of the outcome and how their faith drew countless nurses, doctors, and others they encountered into a captivating story that only our Lord could author.

Cameron Côté, western outreach director for the Canadian Centre for Bio-Ethical Reform and host of *The Pro-Life Guys Podcast*

To my husband, Mau, who has been with me through all the highs and lows. God knew what He was doing when He brought us together. And to Thomas, Nate, and Emma—each one of you is a precious gift from God.

Contents

Introduction

Open your mouth for the speechless,
In the cause of all who are appointed to die.
PROVERBS 31:8, NKJV

The monitor beeps.

I'm propped up on pillows in a hospital maternity ward. Sensors are attached to wires strapped to bands across my protruding belly. A blood pressure cuff is shackled to my right arm. An IV pokes out of my left. I should be in extreme pain this far into labor, but I feel nothing more than a light pressure with each contraction. I marvel at the wonder of the epidural. Other than the discomfort of being confined to this bed, I'm in good spirits, expectant, and hopeful.

I turn my eyes downward and try once again to pick up where I left off in my book, reading and rereading the same paragraph for the third, fourth . . . I've lost count of the number of times. The clock on the wall tells me it's getting late, almost nine thirty. I pause my reading yet again, considering that the long-awaited moment of our hopes, prayers, and fears has almost arrived. The long months of anticipation became weeks, then days, then hours, and they have now dwindled to minutes.

I glance around the hospital room. My husband, Mauricio, is sitting near the bed reading something on his phone. An avid reader, he's spent this time feeding his passion for theology and keeping family and friends updated on my progress. The sky outside is now dark, and the streetlights have come alive on this first day of spring. The smells of disinfectant, clean linens, and musty hallways mingle with the sound of indistinct voices from the hallway outside my room.

Like thrill seekers securely fastened into a roller coaster just beginning its ascent, Mauricio and I have been inching our way toward this day, preparing for the inescapable plunge that we have no way of stopping.

My thoughts drift to the inevitable. Like thrill seekers securely fastened into a roller coaster just beginning its ascent, Mauricio and I have been inching our way toward this day, preparing for the inescapable plunge that we have no way of stopping. We know we're approaching a drop that will take our breath away with its intensity. We steel ourselves for the jarring twists and turns that are sure to shake us and maybe even eject us from the coaster—at least it feels that way. We have no choice but to cling tightly to our seats and to each other, utter desperate prayers for help, and hope that somehow we'll make it through.

We didn't choose to board this ride, and we certainly wish we could get off somehow, but we have faith in the good God who promises to be with us. He's the One who holds us tightly. It's His great and powerful arms that hold us as we hurtle along at breakneck speed. It's to Him we must cling.

Jenny, the nurse who's been monitoring me, enters the room. Her curly red hair is swept up into a tight ponytail. A friendly smile adorns her face.

"Let's take a look here and see how you're doing. I think we must be getting close now," she says as she checks to see how dilated I am. Her relaxed and self-possessed manner helps put me at ease, at least a little bit.

It's Monday, March 20, 2017. This date has been marked on my calendar for several weeks. Moreover, we've been praying that I would make it this far. I'm thirty-eight weeks pregnant with twins, and it's crucial for the babies to be close to full term when they're born—especially "Twin A," as the doctors call him. So here I am. After what seems like forever, I'm about to give birth to two precious babies, thankful to have made it this far.

Examination complete, I look to Jenny, eager for her report. Mauricio stands up and steps to my side.

"You're dilated the full ten centimeters, so . . . it's time," she announces with a twinkle in her eye. "I'll alert Dr. Sharma and the NICU [neonatal intensive care unit] team, and we'll get everyone assembled in the OR [operating room]. I'll be back for you in just a few minutes; then we'll get this show on the road."

We didn't choose to board this ride, and we certainly wish we could get off somehow, but we have faith in the good God who promises to be with us.

Jenny is barely out the door when Mauricio, who's known by family and friends as Mau, takes my hand, his long brown fingers interlacing with my own, and begins to pray: "Lord, thank You for bringing us to this day. We ask You to bless the doctors and nurses as they deliver the babies and to guide everything they do. We pray for Your protection over Christin and the twins, and we ask that You save our little boy. Go before him, and prepare all the care that he requires. We ask this in Jesus' name. Amen."

Mau gazes at me intently, his dark brown eyes filled with a mixture of love and concern, then takes out his iPhone to update his family in Brazil, my family in other parts of Canada, and our church family here in Calgary, Alberta, that the time has come.

Though I should be a mess at this moment, filled with fear and anxiety, I'm actually not. I've never before felt such an odd mixture of excitement, uncertainty, and peace.

PART ONE

"Do You Want to Keep It?"

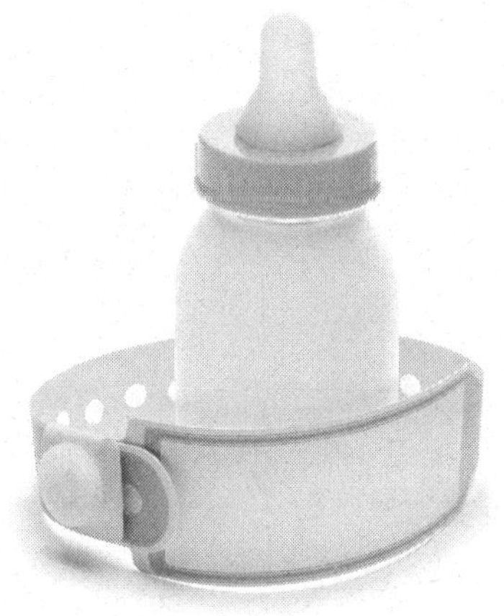

CHAPTER 1

LET THE RIDE BEGIN

Let us hold fast the confession of our hope without wavering, for he who promised is faithful.

HEBREWS 10:23

Mau and I met in Calgary in 2006. Originally from Edmonton—Alberta's provincial capital, some three hours north—I was born into a typical white, middle-class Christian family of five. After graduating with a degree in education from the University of Alberta, I moved to southern China in 2004 to teach English. It was simply something I felt the Lord calling me to do.

I loved my time living on the campus of Shantou University, making friends with students and faculty alike, and traveling throughout Southeast Asia whenever I had a break from school. I loved the tropical climate, fresh fruit, culture, and adventure. But as the second year there started drawing to a close, I knew it was time to return to Canada or I'd never be able to leave my cherished home away from home.

As I began praying for direction, for some reason I sensed that God might bring me to Calgary, though I couldn't imagine why. After all, my parents, sister, and brother all lived in Edmonton, and they were looking forward to my return. I applied for teaching jobs in both cities but was only invited for interviews in Calgary. After receiving a job offer, I found myself in a new city where I knew next to no one.

Mau, also raised in the church, grew up in the giant, concrete, high-rise metropolis of São Paulo, Brazil. The younger of two sons, he grew up in a modest, middle-class home with parents who were both teachers—in many ways a childhood much like my own. After completing his degree in architecture and working in his field for a couple of years, Mau decided to go abroad to take his training to the next level. In 2001 he was accepted into a graduate program in architecture at the University of Calgary, where he devoted himself to his studies and to mastery of the English language.

After completing his master's degree, Mau was invited by his university supervisor to work in the small architectural firm he'd just opened. Although Mau never intended to remain in Canada long term, Calgary became his new home.

Calgary is a midsize city of about 1.5 million people that rests in the foothills of southern Alberta, shadowed to the west by the Rocky Mountains. Calgarians love the outdoors: camping, hiking, skiing, kayaking, skating, swimming, running—every season is another opportunity to enjoy nature. My aunt and uncle graciously hosted me when I first arrived in the summer of 2006—at least until I found a couple of roommates and a house to rent. As I settled into my new living situation and job, come September the realization hit me that I was adjusting to a new city, working a mediocre job, and living life with no real friends. I began to wonder if perhaps I'd misheard God.

God, what am I doing here? Living here just doesn't make any sense. I could be with my family and friends at home, yet I'm here, doing what? I didn't sense any sort of answer to my prayers, so I thought about packing up my belongings and heading back to my *real* home.

+ + +

I'm watching the clock now. It's nine forty. Jenny returns to the room with Dr. Sharma, followed closely by a young intern who is still rather awkward in his bedside manner. Dr. Sharma, on the other hand—middle-aged and beautiful with her glossy black hair—is everything I could hope for in a doctor: competent, efficient, compassionate, unhurried, and trustworthy. I know my babies and I are in expert hands. Equipped with the best resources and medical professionals this city has to offer, this hospital receives all high-risk pregnancies for delivery.

Dr. Sharma flashes Mau and me a reassuring smile.

"Okay, Christin," she says, "we've got the whole team assembled in the OR. As we discussed earlier, the NICU team is there, ready to intubate your baby boy as soon as he's born. Once they have him stabilized, they'll bring him to the NICU. We are hoping to deliver these babies vaginally, but since you're on an epidural, we'll be able to perform a C-section without delay in the event of complications. Your baby boy is in position to be delivered first, followed by your baby girl. Do you two have any questions before we bring you to the OR?"

We shake our heads, and I direct my reply somewhere between her and Mau: "No, I don't think so. I'm ready."

"All right then. We're going to wheel you just across the hall," the doctor says as Jenny unlocks the wheels and begins to move my bed.

Mau washes his hands and puts on a sterile blue hospital gown and cap. Jenny takes a picture of us, both smiling, both giving a thumbs-up. I'm filled with excitement—the wait is almost over!—too much excitement to feel any significant fear. I'm ready to have these babies; I'm ready to find out how this story will unfold.

I'm ready to have these babies; I'm ready to find out how this story will unfold.

My husband, on the other hand, is definitely feeling nervous. Despite all our prayers, we don't know what the coming minutes and hours will hold for our baby boy, and Mau is all too aware that things might not go as we hope.

+ + +

Because I was without a car those first few months in Calgary, I either walked or rode the bus wherever I needed to go. A good friend from Edmonton recommended a church she'd visited that was about a twenty-minute walk from my house, so one overcast September morning I bundled up and made the trek.

The church, located near the University of Calgary, had a robust young-adult ministry. After the morning service, I met a group of single adults who invited me to go out for lunch with them. I was so starved for friendship that I said yes without hesitation. I ended up spending the afternoon with this very welcoming group of guys and girls and then attended a young-adult service back at the church with them that evening. A cheery girl in the group invited me to join a small group that was starting up that coming Thursday. Once again I readily accepted. My thoughts of moving back to Edmonton were beginning to fade.

Little did I know that a young Brazilian architect was also there that evening. He sat a couple of tables away from mine, and though I don't remember noticing him at the time, if you ask him, he'll tell you that I stared at him the whole night. Mau says he was thinking, *Who is this girl, and why is she looking at me?* I must have been gazing in his direction, and we laugh about it now whenever we share the story (much to my embarrassment). After the service, the same cheery girl, already a friend of his, also invited Mau to join the new small group.

The following Thursday evening, eight or nine young adults arrived at the host's home and took a seat in the living room. We studied a passage from the New Testament; I stayed silent, preferring to observe and listen—typical behavior for me in an unfamiliar environment. Mau, on the other hand, shared his thoughts with ease. This immediately impressed me, especially considering that he was speaking in his second language. I had studied Chinese and knew firsthand the challenge of attempting to communicate in a tongue that you're still learning.

After the Bible study concluded and people began to mingle, Mau and I found ourselves chatting.

"So, you're from Brazil?" I asked, fascinated. "I don't actually know much about Brazil; I've never met anyone from there before. What's it like?"

Mau told me a bit about his city and country. "I have a book about Brazil you can borrow if you like."

"I'd like that, thanks!" I replied. "How long have you been in Canada?"

"Three years now. I came here to complete my master's degree in architecture."

The conversation continued, each of us asking questions about the other. He was confident and articulate, his English was excellent, and I could tell he had a strong love for the Lord. I soon learned he was also very kind and often went out of his way to serve others. It didn't take long to recognize that I was interested in him, and it turned out that he was also interested in me. He found it especially intriguing that I had recently returned from China with stories about sharing the gospel with my friends and students there.

The small group welcomed Mau and me wholeheartedly. Most of us were young professionals from various places in western Canada with no other family in town, so we became like family to each other. We got together several times throughout the week, enjoying each other's friendship while doing life together. Mau and I had both found a place of belonging, and I no longer thought about returning to Edmonton. I'd often watch as Mau, joking with the other guys, would burst out in a hearty belly laugh until tears came into his eyes. It was lighthearted and joyful, just like him.

Not knowing how to pronounce his name, we called him Mo-REE-shee-oh, or Mo for short. It was a while before he corrected me: Mao-REE-see-oh. Though I tried to pronounce his name properly, I jumped at the chance to call him Mau after learning it was the nickname he went by with family and friends.

One day in October, Mau invited the whole gang to visit his latest home-design project that was currently under construction. No one was able to go—no one, that is, except me.

+ + +

Even with ten or so people inside, including Mau, the operating room still feels spacious. It's now nine forty-five, and I glance to my right to see the NICU team in their blue gowns, gloves, and masks. Nearby are two contraptions on wheels. I'm guessing that these two white devices are the latest in birthing-room equipment.

The first one is fairly simple—a small, uncovered bassinet with a clean, light-blue pad, two crisply folded sheets, and a sealed package of medical supplies waiting to be opened. What looks like a heat lamp rises up from one end of the bassinet and curves over the top.

The second is an incubator covered in clear plexiglass with two holes on each side that can be opened to attend to the baby. It will keep my baby boy warm and protect him from germs. Inside the plexiglass a striped blanket covers the small mattress pad, and a rolled-up white towel, formed into a U shape, waits to encircle my baby boy's body. Beside it are tubes, monitors, wires, and an oxygen tank.

Mau stands beside me, ready to support me during this delivery and eager to meet his son and daughter. He holds my hand and gives me an encouraging look that speaks volumes. The medical team encircles my bed, all of them dressed in scrubs. Dr. Sharma introduces me to the young man next to her.

"This is Dr. Connor," she says. "He's a resident here and will be assisting me with the delivery today."

I nod and smile, a bit surprised. I feel like I have somehow stumbled onto the set of a medical drama—both these doctors are uncommonly attractive. I'm so accustomed to watching fictional characters like this on TV that it's surprising such good-looking doctors actually exist.

"On your next contraction I want you to push," instructs Dr. Sharma, bringing my attention back to the matter at hand. She and Dr. Connor are side by side, prepared to catch Nathaniel while still keeping an eye on the monitors.

"Okay, Christin—push!"

+ + +

Mau picked me up and drove us to the construction site. There, on a crisp fall afternoon, he gave me the grand tour. I must admit that I was dazzled, quite impressed that the guy from my small group had designed this stunning contemporary home. After the tour we decided to get some food, and we found a chic Indian restaurant nearby. Our conversation flowed so effortlessly that, before we realized it, it was ten o'clock and we were the last customers in the place. I was completely smitten with this handsome, intelligent, godly man. From that time forward, we spent more and more time together.

We officially started dating in February 2007 and were married in July 2008. We had a traditional wedding in Edmonton, surrounded by family and friends, just as I had always dreamed. The ceremony was held downtown surrounded by the stunning stained-glass windows of First Baptist Church and was followed by a reception at the renowned Northern Alberta Jubilee Auditorium. One of the most memorable parts of the ceremony was when we sang the classic hymn "Great Is Thy Faithfulness":

Great is Thy faithfulness!
Great is Thy faithfulness!
Morning by morning new mercies I see;

All I have needed Thy hand hath provided.
Great is Thy faithfulness, Lord, unto me!

My twenty-six-year-old self marveled at God's faithfulness in bringing me such an admirable man, but I had yet to grasp a deep understanding of how the Lord remains faithful even when one's world is shattered—an understanding that can only come through hardship. Not knowing what the future held yet still full of hope, two lives came together that day, committing in the sight of God to love and care for each other through the highs and lows, for better or for worse, unaware at the time how the lows yet to come would eventually threaten to outweigh the highs. Nine years into our marriage, we would experience the biggest "for worse" we had ever encountered.

+ + +

I begin pushing with all my might. Well, I *hope* that's what I'm doing. I honestly can't feel much of anything thanks to the epidural, but I hope something's happening. The contraction wanes, and I catch my breath.

"Good job, Christin!" says Dr. Sharma. "Okay, we're going to do this again. Here comes the next contraction."

I push again, trying to remember to breathe.

"Great job! Keep going—we can see his head!"

The contraction ends, and another soon begins. I push like I've never pushed before.

"That's it. That's it! Here he comes!" Dr. Sharma exclaims.

I glance down to see Dr. Connor ready to catch my baby in his hands, Dr. Sharma at his side.

This is the moment—the moment before my life changes forever, the moment Mau and I have been waiting for with a stew of emotions. It's that point on a roller coaster when you seem to hang in the air, just before the drop. You've strapped yourself into your seat and made the agonizing ascent filled with a mixture of exhilaration and fear. There's no turning back now, no getting off, no way out. You've reached the apex; there's nothing above you, nothing ahead but empty sky, and you can only wait—wait for the dramatic plunge.

There's no turning back now, no getting off, no way out.

You think maybe, just maybe, the drop might not come and you might avoid what waits ahead, but then your world begins to tilt forward, downward, as your reality once again comes frighteningly into view. So you brace yourself by grabbing onto a bar, or belt, or strap—whatever is available—with a white-knuckled grip. You know full well that there's no stopping now.

Push.

Let the ride begin.

CHAPTER 2

FROM INFERTILITY TO DOUBLE BLESSING

"For this child I prayed, and the Lord *has granted me my petition that I made to him."*
1 SAMUEL 1:27

Mau and I waited five years before trying to start our family. I was beyond ready to begin sooner, but it took Mau a bit longer before he agreed that we were prepared for the demands of parenthood. Finally, after a year and a half of trying without success, to our great delight I became pregnant, and I gave birth to Thomas in July 2013.

Eight months later, Mau made the decision to leave architecture and move into full-time ministry with Promise Keepers Canada (now called Impactus). After setting up his new home office, our family of three settled into a happy rhythm of work and play and togetherness, delighting in each new milestone with our little boy.

Just before Thomas turned two, Mau and I decided to start trying for a second child. We were hopeful that I would conceive more easily the second time, but after six months of trying with no results, we found ourselves at a fertility clinic. We sat in a waiting room filled with other hopeful couples, then moved to a smaller room, where we sat across from a doctor who was reviewing our file.

"Most couples in your situation consider a treatment called intrauterine insemination, otherwise known as IUI," she said. She proceeded to explain the process, which is simpler than in vitro fertilization (IVF) and much less costly. "We would prescribe medication for you, Christin, to stimulate ovulation and thereby increase your chances of conceiving. There's a 13 percent chance of success with each treatment. We recommend that couples try the treatment at least three times before considering other options, but it's ultimately up to you to decide."

Only a 13 percent chance of becoming pregnant, I thought. *Those aren't very good odds.* But then I remembered all those reality shows about families who've had sextuplets. I couldn't help but wonder if something similar could happen to us.

"What's the likelihood that we'd have multiples?" I asked.

"Not very likely at all," the doctor replied. "Of the 13 percent of women who conceive with each treatment, only 7 percent of those women have multiples."

We discussed our options on the car ride home.

"So what do you think?" I asked Mau.

He let out a sigh. "I love the idea of adoption," he said. "It's just too bad that it's such a long and complicated process."

Adoption pamphlets sat on a table at home, the research process already begun. "I think it wouldn't hurt to try IUI first," he added, "just to rule out pregnancy."

I nodded. "I agree. And if it's unsuccessful, we can pursue adoption all out." I paused as I thought about recent news reports. "We should wait until we get back from Brazil in April. I wouldn't want to risk getting the Zika virus if I was already pregnant by then."

"Right," Mau agreed. "Well, sounds like we have a plan."

We'd already made plans to visit Mau's family for three weeks, this time along with my parents, Dan and Nancy, and my sister, Jaci. The Public Health Agency of Canada had advised pregnant women to postpone travel to countries—such as Brazil—where Zika was present. The virus can pass from a pregnant woman to her preborn baby, potentially causing microcephaly and severe brain malformations. I wasn't thrilled with the prospect of more waiting, but I would never risk the health of my baby.

The thought that continued to swirl in my brain popped out in conversation. "My only fear is that we're going to end up with quadruplets," I said to Mau. "I know the chance of multiples is low, but I'm not convinced there's anything medically wrong with us. God gave us Thomas without any medical intervention, right? If I take this medication, what if we end up with multiples? I know children are a gift from the Lord, but I just don't know if I'd be able to take care of four babies!"

"Christin," Mau said calmly, "don't get ahead of yourself. Don't worry. We'll pray about it and trust that the Lord will work out all the details."

He promptly put the idea out of his mind, but I couldn't quite shake the possibility of multiples.

After returning from South America, we took a blood test that confirmed we didn't have the Zika virus, so we made an appointment to have our first fertility treatment in June.

Unfortunately, nothing went as it was supposed to. I used a special kit to determine when I was ovulating, but I never got a positive result. Next, the clinic instructed me to inject myself with a medication at home that should make me ovulate. But when the time came to give myself the injection, I had trouble following the poorly written instructions. I was shaking and flustered, unsure whether I was doing it correctly. Not surprisingly, that treatment also failed.

My experience the following month, however, was like night and day compared to that. Everything went as it should. I got a very clear positive result indicating that I was ovulating, and the treatment seemed to work. A few days after celebrating Thomas's third birthday, it was time to take the pregnancy test. Positive! Mau and I were filled with relief and jubilation, thrilled that Thomas was going to be a big brother.

Unfortunately, nothing went as it was supposed to.

In August 2016, I made an appointment to see my family physician. Dr. Martinez was young, competent, personable, and thorough. Since moving to Calgary, I'd bounced from one doctor to another, never quite satisfied with the care I'd received, until a medical clinic close to home had opened up and begun accepting new patients. I found myself with the first female doctor I'd ever had, and she'd been a breath of fresh air.

Until now.

Dr. Martinez had been traveling this second journey of infertility along with me. In fact, she was the one who had referred me to the fertility clinic. I was eager to tell her my good news as I waited in the examination room.

She entered the room and took a seat on a stool in front of me.

"How are you?" she asked warmly. "What can I do for you today?"

"Well . . . I'm pregnant!" I beamed. And then, like getting a punch in the gut that leaves you gasping for air, I was caught off guard by her next words.

"Do you want to keep it?" she asked without missing a beat.

Am I hearing her correctly? I wondered. *Is she suggesting what I think she is? Doesn't she know that we've been trying to have a child? Doesn't she know that my baby is a treasure and already loved? Doesn't she know that of course I want to keep my child, that there's no question and never will be a question that I want to keep my child?*

As often seems to happen, my reply didn't come out quite the way I wanted. I furrowed my brow, perplexed. "Well, yes—I've been trying to get pregnant . . ."

"Okay, I just have to ask," she responded matter-of-factly. "And would you like to have a nuchal translucency screen?"

Another unexpected question. Though I wasn't exactly sure what a nuchal translucency screen was—I'd only heard of an amniocentesis—I figured it was one of the tests done early on in a pregnancy to determine whether there's a chance the baby has Down syndrome or other genetic conditions. I was also aware that many mothers who take this test, though not all, would consider aborting their child depending on the results. I know many people believe that it's better not to have such children, which is one reason I've always associated genetic testing with abortion. I didn't need to think about my answer.

"No," I replied.

Not everyone realizes that genetic testing isn't always accurate and has definite limitations. I'm certainly not a medical professional, but numerous studies have revealed that false positive results commonly occur in nuchal translucency screens, even when combined with a noninvasive prenatal test (NIPT).[1] An NIPT can reliably determine the presence of some conditions, but there are many conditions it can't detect. NIPTs are even prone to produce false positives for a few rare genetic conditions. Some doctors express misgivings about offering these tests because they can cause undue stress in their patients and also promote discrimination toward those currently living with disabilities. Another concern is the commonly held misconception that these tests diagnose genetic conditions when in fact they merely assess their possible *likelihood*.[2]

I knew none of this information during my appointment with Dr. Martinez. All I knew was that I wasn't interested in learning whether my child might have a genetic condition. It definitely wouldn't change my mind about whether I would continue with my pregnancy. Dr. Martinez printed out a requisition for an ultrasound and handed it to me. I planned to make an appointment once I returned home. She then excused herself and left the room without explanation, returning several minutes later.

"I just consulted with a colleague because I wanted to get a second opinion," Dr. Martinez said. "She and I both feel it's important that you consider doing the nuchal translucency test. Are you sure you don't want to do it?"

I was stunned. I'd come to this appointment completely unprepared for the stark difference in perspective between me and my doctor. I didn't know if this insistence for patients to undergo genetic testing was common practice with all doctors, but my faith in Dr. Martinez was shaken.

"Yes, I'm sure," I said.

+ + +

Before that appointment, I had never personally confronted the issue of abortion. The topic had rarely come up in conversation when I was growing up. We never talked about it at home. We never talked about it at school. We never talked about it in church. Yet somehow I knew what it was, and somehow I knew it was wrong.

At about ten years old, I began reading the Bible daily. As I read, God's Word began to instruct my heart and feed my soul. I eventually came across Psalm 139 and learned that God is always with me no matter where I go and that He knows everything about me because He is my Creator. And in verses 13-16, I read words that have become dear to me:

> You formed my inward parts;
> you knitted me together in my mother's womb.
> I praise you, for I am fearfully and wonderfully made.
> Wonderful are your works;
> my soul knows it very well.
> My frame was not hidden from you,
> when I was being made in secret,
> intricately woven in the depths of the earth.
> Your eyes saw my unformed substance;
> in your book were written, every one of them,
> the days that were formed for me,
> when as yet there was none of them.
>
> PSALM 139:13-16

By God's grace, and without any specific training, I realized that I had been precious to God and *known* by God even before I was born. I came to the conclusion that if this was true for me, it was also true for *everyone*.

I was fourteen when I participated in perhaps my only conversation about abortion prior to adulthood. During a sleepover with some friends from school, as we sat in my friend's basement, two of the girls argued that abortion in the case of rape was justifiable, while my best friend and I attempted (not very successfully) to articulate that killing an unborn child was never justifiable. All I knew was that a baby is a baby and that no child—regardless of the circumstances of their conception—should be sentenced to death. Nor should the mother have to endure another trauma in addition to her rape.

I realized that I had been precious to God and known *by God even before I was born.*

The closest I ever came to anyone who had experienced an unplanned pregnancy or who was considering terminating a pregnancy was a single conversation I overheard while riding the bus home from high school. Of the two girls who sat behind me, I recognized only one; she lived in my neighborhood and was a couple of years younger than me. As I looked out the bus window watching houses pass by, I heard her say in a whisper, "My period is late. I think I might be pregnant." She sounded so young, so vulnerable. I never saw her again, but I've always wondered: Was she pregnant? Did she have the baby, or did she . . . ? How is she doing today? I know many women face very difficult circumstances, and I can understand why abortion might seem like their only option. My heart goes out to them.

Abortion had long been a mystery to me—an apparition shrouded in a mist of secrecy that few were willing to talk about openly. I had no idea where or how it was done. I had no idea what laws (if any) regulated it. I had no concept of the emotional, physical, or spiritual implications for those involved. I knew next to nothing. And before my appointment with Dr. Martinez, abortion was always someone else's concern—not mine.

But now it *was* mine. Someone—a respected medical professional—just asked (no, *encouraged*) me to do genetic testing on my unborn baby. She didn't say it explicitly, but the unspoken assumption was that a positive result would suggest *termination*. But how could I consider that when God already saw my developing child? There was nothing random about the life growing within me. My child was loved beyond measure regardless of any potential birth defects, and Mau and I intended to do everything possible to protect this life.

Someone—a respected medical professional—just asked (no, encouraged*) me to do genetic testing on my unborn baby. She didn't say it explicitly, but the unspoken assumption was that a positive result would* suggest termination.

+ + +

In the weeks and months that followed my appointment with Dr. Martinez, I began to wonder why she'd asked if I wanted to keep the baby. *Are doctors trained to ask this question? And if so, why?*

I realized that I'd been insulated from these questions and their implications for most of my life. What did most doctors believe about abortion and the unborn? And what about society as a whole? I was sure about my own beliefs regarding the rights and value of unborn children, but what did others believe?

I'd never considered such questions during my pregnancy with Thomas, largely because I'd spent the first several months of that period in Brazil. There I'd had regular checkups with an obstetrician who was devoted to the care of both mother and baby. That's part of the reason I was caught off guard by my initial appointment with my Canadian doctor, never guessing that my second pregnancy was just the beginning of the greatest trial Mau and I had ever encountered.

A good friend of mine practiced medicine back in Edmonton, so I asked about her medical-school training regarding these questions. She said the topic of abortion was somewhat taboo at her medical school, that perspectives varied among hospitals and individual physicians, and that it was often only mentioned in passing. Whenever the topic came up in medical school for her, it was typically discussed in a sensitive manner, with the understanding that people have differing views. She was taught to ask if patients wanted the nuchal translucency screen and that it was recommended but also that it shouldn't be pushed on patients.

As I thought about my friend's words, I couldn't help but wonder: *Do all medical schools follow the same approach? If abortion is supposedly a normal medical procedure, why is the topic taboo for those training to be doctors? Why would there be differing views requiring such sensitivity for a so-called normal medical procedure? And why wouldn't the discussion surrounding this topic be standardized?*

I later learned that Canada hasn't had any laws governing abortion since 1988. None. Not one. This essentially means that all abortions, from conception to birth, are perfectly legal. And not just legal but also fully funded by Canada's public healthcare system. Each province makes their own rules regarding how far into pregnancy they will allow and fund abortion, but all provinces provide free access to abortion.[3]

When Canada became a nation in 1867, abortion was illegal and remained so for more than one hundred years—until legislation was passed in 1969 that permitted abortions only if a committee of doctors determined that a woman's life or health was in danger. But things changed dramatically in 1988. In the case *R. v. Morgentaler*, the Supreme Court of Canada ruled that the existing law was unconstitutional based on the *Canadian Charter of Rights and Freedoms*. When the 1969 law was struck down, it was assumed that Parliament would implement new legislation to provide clarity, yet no such law has ever been passed.[4]

Moreover, in my country, babies are only considered human beings once they have completely exited the birth canal, thus abortions can be performed on partially born children.[5] Abortion continues to be a taboo subject in most sectors of Canadian society, and politicians who call for limitations on this practice are very likely to have short political careers—scorned by colleagues, the media, and many (but not all) ordinary citizens. Though the majority of abortions are performed during the first trimester and many doctors refuse to perform late-term abortions, the fact remains that abortion at any stage is perfectly legal throughout Canada.

My appointment with Dr. Martinez behind me, I looked forward to the ultrasound that would help determine our baby's due date. I envisioned another happy and healthy pregnancy just like the one I'd enjoyed with Thomas.

Mau came with me on August 29 to the medical diagnostic imaging center. We entered a darkened room that contained an examination bed and a medical technician. I'd been instructed to drink four cups of water before arriving at the appointment, so I was trying hard to ignore my growing discomfort. The technician applied warm ultrasound gel to my belly, and all three of us gazed intently at the monitor.

I was about to ask the question that had been on my mind since we'd first considered IUI when the tech quipped, "I see two little beans in there."

Two little beans! I was right—I'd long suspected that we'd have more than one baby, but I was in a state of utter disbelief that my suspicion was now reality. *Us? Parents of twins? No way!* I couldn't help but laugh out of a combination of incredulity and joy.

Mau, on the other hand, was silent. Probably because he was in complete disbelief. Despite my hunch, he'd never seriously considered the possibility of multiples. I noticed tears glistening in his eyes as he, too, laughed nervously. As the initial shock began to wear off, elation and gratitude took their rightful place. We had hit the jackpot, and luck had had nothing to do with it.

The babies were due at the beginning of April 2017. Let the preparations begin! On the short car ride home, we were already discussing the preparations we'd need to make for twins. For example, where would Mau work? His home office was in our third bedroom, which we'd now need for the twins. Would we need to move? Would we need to buy another car—one big enough to fit three car seats? Would Mau need to find a better-paying job? He worked in full-time ministry, in a job he loved, but *two* additional children would be expensive, right? We began to pray for wisdom and direction. How were we going to make this work?

Us? Parents of twins? No way!

CHAPTER 3

SHATTERED HOPE

"For my thoughts are not your thoughts,
neither are your ways my ways, declares the LORD.
For as the heavens are higher than the earth,
so are my ways higher than your ways
and my thoughts than your thoughts."

ISAIAH 55:8-9

As the weeks went by, God gave us wisdom and answers to many of our questions.

I measured the back seat of our car and went looking for the narrowest car seats on the market. I discovered that two infant seats and Thomas's toddler seat would just fit—it would be snug, but we wouldn't have to buy a new car. Our church offered Mau the unused corner of a basement storage room to set up his office. It didn't have a window or the best ventilation, but we now had a free bedroom at home for the twins. We determined that our current house and Mau's salary would be enough; we could make do with careful budgeting, just as we always had. Little by little, the preparations for our expanded family were coming together.

I was looking forward to my eighteen-week ultrasound appointment with the vibrating anticipation of a child waiting for Christmas morning. Ever since we learned we were having twins, we'd been thinking about the possible combinations. Two boys? Two girls? One of each? Thomas said he wanted two boys named Thomas Two and Thomas Three. Of course we agreed that we'd be pleased with any combination, but we concluded that a boy and a girl would be ideal. That way Thomas would have both a brother and a sister, and the twins would likely enjoy a special bond of their own.

Before the appointment Mau sent a playful group message to his family in Brazil asking them to make their predictions regarding the big gender reveal. I did the same on Facebook. It never once occurred to us that this appointment could be anything but joyous. How blissfully oblivious we were.

November 3 arrived, and we once again entered a darkened examination room. I again felt the familiar warmth of the ultrasound gel and again watched the grainy black-and-white images moving on the screen. I heard the familiar *wom wom wom* of one heartbeat and then the other. As the technician moved the transducer over my belly, I tried to make sense of the images.

With a cry of delight I exclaimed, "It's a girl!"

"You've got a good eye," replied the tech. "Yes, congratulations—you're having a girl."

I'd always wanted a little girl, and I was filled with gratitude and thankfulness toward God. Mau held my hand, and we grinned at each other.

A minute later the tech announced, "You're also having a boy."

Mau and I were thrilled. A boy and a girl, just as we'd been hoping!

The technician methodically took picture after picture for several more minutes. We basked in the joy of the moment. She informed us that she needed a doctor to take a look at the results and come speak with us. We thought nothing of it. After all, my pregnancy with Thomas had progressed without a hitch. We had both been the picture of health from start to finish. I didn't realize that the purpose of this routine prenatal ultrasound was not just to learn the babies' genders but also to screen for fetal abnormalities.

We were still absorbing the wonderful news about our boy and girl when the radiologist entered the room. He took a seat near the door. "I'm sorry to inform you that we have detected a condition in Twin A called congenital diaphragmatic hernia, otherwise known as CDH."

Wait. What?

"I'm going to refer you to a special clinic for women with high-risk pregnancies. They'll take over your prenatal care going forward, and I'd like you to see them next week. I've already sent over a referral, so you should receive a call from them in the next day or so to set up the appointment."

And that was it. He answered a couple of basic questions and gave us the business card of the clinic. Mau and I left the appointment feeling somewhat confused. We had no substantial information other than the name of the condition, nor did we have any idea of its severity. We hoped our next appointment would prove this diagnosis to be but a minor blip, easily resolved. We asked the Lord to heal our little boy, and I believed in my heart of hearts that He would. I didn't yet understand that God had a bigger plan for our family—a plan that required more than a quick fix.

November 9 found Mau and me at the special maternity clinic. The two curved six-story buildings mirrored each other like a circle cut down the middle, attached only by a shared lobby. As I scanned the structure for the first time, I had no idea that I would eventually lose track of the number of visits I'd make to this place.

On the fourth floor we were greeted by a chic, gold silhouette of a pregnant woman posted prominently on the wall. The decor was clean and elegant. The mixture of gray rock, fresh white paint, and natural wood tones was inviting. Light flooded in through large windows, and fresh scents lingered in the air. The soft chatter of waiting couples and small children floated around us.

From all appearances, the clinic gave every indication of providing quality healthcare. But appearances can be deceiving. The polished veneer of our surroundings masked the true colors of this place.

An ultrasound technician called out my name. We followed the young woman down a seemingly endless hallway, past several doors, around a corner, and past yet more doors. We trailed behind her like two lost travelers venturing into the bowels of a cave. At last we came to her room. In the dim light she began what would be a two-hour-long detailed ultrasound, deftly capturing image after image, measurement after measurement. As I looked at Twin A and Twin B on the monitor, to my untrained eye they both looked perfectly normal.

From all appearances, the clinic gave every indication of providing quality healthcare. But appearances can be deceiving.

The technician did her job in almost complete silence. At long last she stepped out of the room to inform the doctor that the scan was complete. We were taken to a consultation room to wait.

I was actually thankful for the reprieve after that lengthy exam. Mau and I sat there together—hoping for the best, unprepared for the worst.

A doctor eventually entered the room. She introduced herself and told us that our little boy did in fact have congenital diaphragmatic hernia. She spoke slowly and carefully.

"Let me explain CDH," she said. "CDH occurs when the diaphragm—the muscle that separates the chest from the abdomen—doesn't close properly during prenatal development. The hole in the diaphragm allows the organs of the abdomen—such as the kidneys, intestines, stomach, and liver—to migrate into the chest. When this happens, these abdominal organs crowd out the lungs and impact their growth and development."

She paused before summing up the situation. "When a baby with severe CDH is born, they can't breathe because their lungs are too small."

She went on to explain that these small lungs have less-developed blood vessels, which causes high blood pressure in the lungs, known as pulmonary hypertension. We also learned that CDH is one of the most common major congenital anomalies, occurring in about one out of every twenty-five hundred to three thousand live births.[1]

"We just completed a high-resolution fetal ultrasound," the doctor said, "and we can see that the liver and some of the intestines have moved through the hole on the right side of the diaphragm and have pushed the fetus's lungs and heart to the left. The left lung is quite small, while the right lung is almost nonexistent."

I felt like my senses were under assault. I struggled to take it all in, to process everything she was saying. It was dawning on me that this diagnosis was no small matter. Disbelief turned to despair.

It turns out that the strongest predictor of CDH's severity is the location of the liver. When the liver is located in the chest, as in our baby boy's case, the result is smaller lungs and thus a more serious condition. Doctors compare the size of the larger lung—our baby's left lung—and the size of the baby's head using ultrasound. From these measurements they can determine the lung-to-head ratio (LHR), which is used to predict survival. The ultrasound results revealed that our baby's lung-to-head ratio was 27 percent, meaning that the left lung was just 27 percent of the size of a healthy lung in relation to the head. Needless to say, our boy's percentage was quite low.

What did that mean for us? "We would predict a 25- to 50-percent survival rate, but realistically it's closer to 25 percent," the doctor explained. She paused, lines of concern etching her brow. "To give you some perspective, even with treatment, very few babies survive when the lung-to-head ratio is 25 percent or less."

"We would predict a 25-to 50-percent survival rate, but realistically it's closer to 25 percent," the doctor explained.

That's all—25 percent? What does this mean for our little boy? I can't believe this is really happening. It felt surreal. *This can't be my baby she's talking about.*

She also informed us that survivors of CDH often go on to have other health concerns, such as pulmonary hypertension, asthma, developmental disabilities, scoliosis, feeding disorders, hearing loss, and gastrointestinal reflux.

So there it was. Such a bleak outlook for our beloved boy—a child for whom we had such hopes and dreams. It was a lot of information to absorb, and I wasn't sure what to think. I was in a state of dismay—no, a state of shock. We had entered the clinic that day with a naïve sense of hope, but now I was descending into a waking nightmare. I looked over at Mau, and I could see from the look of concentration on his face that he was assessing the situation.

What was he thinking?

+ + +

Chug, chug, chug . . .

Beep, beep, beep . . .

Mau's here! I thought with a laugh as I ran to the window in time to see him back his old beater into the driveway. I threw on my shoes and jacket and grabbed my purse.

It was a cool Saturday in the fall of 2006, and Mau and I were headed out for the day. We weren't officially dating yet, but we'd been spending a lot of time together. I knew I liked him, and let me just say that it wasn't due to his flashy ride! (Who's ever heard of a sedan that beeps when it backs up?) Mau wanted to introduce me to some friends of his from back home in Brazil. They had recently moved to a town near Calgary to attend Bible college, not realizing at the time how close they would be to Mau.

The drive to that town afforded us a spectacular view of the foothills at the base of the towering Canadian Rockies. Mau's friends, Gustavo and Bianca, welcomed us into their cozy student residence with big smiles and hugs and kisses. Even though we'd just met, I still received the customary Brazilian greeting.

"This is Bia, and this is Luisa," Gustavo said with pride as he gathered into his arms his two- and three-year-old daughters, both of them looking at me with big, shy eyes. "And these"—he gestured—"are the twins!"

There, side by side in matching infant seats, were two identical newborn boys.

Twins? I can't even imagine! This couple sure has their hands full.

Bianca beamed at me and, through broken English, told me their names and asked if I wanted to hold one of the boys. How could I refuse? Inexperienced with babies as I was, I held one stiffly in my arms as Bianca prepared food in the kitchen.

A couple of weeks earlier, Mau had lent me a book about Brazil. When my junior high class had studied Brazil in social studies, all I remembered learning was that the Amazon rainforests were at risk of disappearing within twenty years if people didn't stop cutting the trees to make way for more farmland. To my amazement, I realized that Brazil was also a country of large, modern cities and was rich with culture (yet not without its challenges). Its people speak Portuguese, love the beach, eat rice and beans, drink coffee, and perform samba music and dance. I learned that lunch is the main meal of the day in Brazilian culture. Finally, I discovered that Brazil has a history of slavery that wasn't abolished until 1888.[2] I found all of it fascinating.

My future was now in session.

"Your friends are great," I remarked to Mau as we drove away. "Can you teach me some Portuguese?"

"Sure," Mau said. "What do you want to know?"

"How do you say, 'Hello, how are you?'"

"*Oi, tudo bem?*" (pronounced "*Oy, tudu bain?*"). I tried it out a few times.

"How about 'Thank you'?" I asked.

My future was now in session.

+ + +

"Given the severity of the fetus's condition," the doctor continued, "there are certain options that you might want to consider. You might like to consider having a reduction. We can refer you to the services you'd require should you make that decision."

The doctor was speaking in a straightforward and soothing manner, but I detected some uneasiness as she attempted to tread lightly.

"This is a time-sensitive matter," she said, "because we would need to do the procedure no later than twenty-two weeks."

Once again I was completely caught off guard by a doctor's words. Like a deer caught in the headlights, I could barely think. We'd just been given a devastating diagnosis, one that was a lot to digest, and then this doctor was suggesting . . . what? *Is she saying what I think she is?* Before even discussing our baby's treatment options, was she suggesting that we end his life? And what were these words she used? *Procedure*? *Reduction*?

I was thankful that Mau was with me, thankful that we have the same convictions even though we hadn't had a moment to discuss the situation, and thankful for his strength. Mau is never intimidated about speaking the truth and calling things out, even if it makes others uncomfortable.

"We realize that you're talking about abortion," he said, speaking calmly and clearly. "Are you suggesting that we abort our little boy? What about our little girl? Would she be put at risk?" I know he was asking merely for the sake of understanding, not because he was actually considering the suggested course of action.

"Ah, yes," the doctor replied, "a reduction would involve the removal of Twin A only." She was doing her best to hide her uneasiness. "There's a good chance that there would be no adverse effects to Twin B, but of course the procedure always comes with risk."

"I see," Mau said. "Well, you need to know that a reduction, as you call it, is not an option for us—even if there were no risk to our little girl. We choose life for our little boy. As long as we can fight for him, we will."

He spoke politely and with a firmness that I admired, though I'm ashamed to admit that I felt a bit embarrassed by his forthrightness. I'm much quieter—still quite firm in my convictions, but less prone to voice them unless I feel comfortable in a situation. I tend to think deeply about things that matter to me, but often I'm not able to articulate my thoughts as well as I'd like to, as clear as they are in my own head.

"We choose life for our little boy," Mau said. "As long as we can fight for him, we will."

The doctor shifted in her seat with visible discomfort, unsure of what to say next. She nodded slowly and told us that she heard us. She then asked us to wait while she arranged for us to meet with the head of the clinic, Dr. Blair.

+ + +

Perhaps to this doctor we were an oddity. But we couldn't be the only couple in this situation who refused even the suggestion of a *reduction*—could we? Then again, I imagine we must have been one of very few. I know most Canadians go along with the status quo. To them, the issue of abortion in Canada is settled. A given. And from a legal perspective, they're right. Most of them have grown up in a nation where abortion is normal, where many have never questioned it or even considered the hard reality of the practice. And when someone dares to bring up the issue, most Canadians would rather change the subject. They'd rather not be reminded of their own regrets or trauma. They don't want to rock the boat. They don't want a revolution. That's just not the Canadian way.

Yet what about those Canadians who do question or even oppose abortion? Why don't they say anything? What emotions guide them? For some the answer is fear—fear of standing out from the crowd. Fear of being ostracized. Fear of being vulnerable about their own pasts. Fear holds people back. It shackles us. It keeps us silent. For others the answer is loneliness, the thought of being outnumbered, part of a tiny minority. It's the feeling of not knowing what to say or do or how to make a difference. It's a feeling that can lead to hopelessness and continued inaction.

I know without a doubt that it's much harder to be pro-life in Canada than in America. In Canada we can hardly engage in open dialogue. In Calgary, for example, pro-lifers aren't allowed to speak to women or even pray within fifty meters of an abortion clinic.[3] While these restrictions have been approved in the name of promoting "community peace," it's the babies and their mothers who get no peace as a result of the forced silence.

In fact, I've seen how promoting this sort of peace actually leads to heartache. I know a woman who, when she attended college in Canada several years ago, was part of a small class of twenty students—two guys and eighteen girls. One day the class discussion turned to abortion, and this young woman was the lone voice representing the pro-life cause. She spoke up for the rights of the preborn and the well-being of the women involved. The conversation was so animated that the professor extended the class time to allow for continued discussion.

To the young woman's astonishment, throughout the following week sixteen of the other women from her class sought her out and revealed their secret: They had each had at least one abortion, and they all felt regret. In public many Canadians want to avoid the topic, but in private they acknowledge that abortion leaves lasting wounds—both physical and emotional—even if they're reluctant to talk about them.

And what of the situation in Brazil? In 1890 the nation criminalized abortion in all circumstances, at least until 1940, when provisions were made for legal abortions in the case of rape and incest or when a woman's life was in danger. These laws remain in effect to this day.[4] During Mau's teenage and young-adult years, he and his friends had discussed it on a philosophical level, in the same way they might have discussed the dangers of drug use. It would seem that the issue of abortion in Mau's native land is also settled.

If only it were so.

In recent years there has been a strong push to legalize abortion in Brazil, and illicit clinics are now plentiful. Though abortion in most cases remains illegal on paper, as many as four million abortions are performed in Brazil each year.[5] This is in a nation with a population of about 212 million people.[6] Compare that to America's estimated one million abortions per year[7] in a country with a population of more than 340 million people.[8]

+ + +

Sitting in a plush leather chair in Dr. Blair's office, I wondered why we needed to meet with yet another doctor. Was she going to give us more information about what would happen next? Maybe only couples who decided to go forward with their pregnancies needed to see the head of the clinic.

I admit that I wasn't expecting the young woman who greeted us. The clinic chief looked to be in her midthirties, about the same age as me. Dressed with impeccable taste, unassuming and down-to-earth, Dr. Blair projected a demeanor of kindness instead of the arrogance some doctors convey. We had barely met, but part of me liked her already.

"I understand that you'd like to move forward with the pregnancy," she said with an expression that suggested both compassion and sympathy. She paused as we nodded. "I need to make sure you understand that the outlook for Twin A is not promising. We can make no guarantee that the fetus will survive—the odds are very low. Are you sure you won't consider a reduction?"

"We're well aware that our little boy might not make it," Mau replied, "and that the odds are not in his favor, but we'll fight for his life nevertheless. To answer your question, no, we won't consider a reduction. It's not up to us to decide whether he should live, so we're going to leave that decision in God's hands. We just ask that you do everything in your power to help save him."

Dr. Blair must think we're either in denial or religious freaks, I thought, but I knew better. It's true that we were likely in a state of shock, and we definitely hadn't had a chance to process this devastating diagnosis, but we were both educated, grounded adults who understood the implications of what we'd been told. Our decision was motivated by convictions we'd embraced years before. We knew that the babies in my womb were already very much alive; they weren't tumors or mere clumps of cells to be removed without a second thought. They already possessed beating hearts, moving limbs, growing organs, and unique DNA. But they were also vulnerable, and as their parents, God had given us the important job of protecting them.

We also believed that if the Creator of the universe could form the vast expanse of space, along with endless galaxies filled with infinite stars and planets, then could He not save our son if He so chose? If we took matters into our own hands and ended our baby's life, would we not be playing God? We can't tell Him what to do, nor can we always understand why He does what He does, but we can cry out to Him and hold on to hope. By letting God decide the outcome of our son's life, we found a different kind of freedom.

We knew that the babies in my womb were already very much alive; they weren't tumors or mere clumps of cells to be removed without a second thought.

We concluded that it wasn't our choice to make. We didn't have to carry the burden of deciding to end our son's life, nor the pain of living with that decision's consequences. Instead we were filled with an inexplicable peace. We were free.

"Given your decision," the doctor said, "let me tell you what you can expect going forward. First of all, we don't know yet if we'll be able to operate when Twin A is born. It all depends on the size of the lungs. Because those lungs are currently very underdeveloped, it's extremely important that the twins are close to full term when they're born in order to move forward with treatment. Twin A needs as much time as possible in utero for the lungs to develop, thereby increasing the chance of survival at birth."

Her words were a revelation. This was the first time anyone had actually mentioned *treating* our little boy, and I was thrilled to hear that it was at least a consideration. I also learned that I'd be returning to this same clinic every two weeks for regular ultrasounds to track both babies' development.

Dr. Blair described what we could expect for the twins' birth, assuming they didn't come early. Because Thomas was born by natural delivery, I shouldn't require a C-section. Their plan, the doctor said, was to induce the twins' birth at thirty-eight weeks.

"Immediately after birth," she said, "our highly trained team will take charge of Twin A. They'll be in the delivery room, ready to intubate him. Then they'll take him to the NICU to be stabilized. As soon as he is stable enough, we'll transfer him by ambulance to the city's children's hospital, where he'll stay for the remainder of his treatment. This transfer will likely take place a day or two after he's born.

"It will be stressful for him, so we'll need to wait again several days until he's stable enough to withstand surgery. A surgeon will move his liver and intestines down into his abdomen and correct the hernia. Do you have any questions?"

It was a lot to process, Mau admitted. "I think the takeaway for me is that our little boy needs to be full-term to have the best chance of survival."

"Yes, that's right," Dr. Blair replied.

"Actually, there is something I want to ask," Mau said. "After our appointment last week, I did a little research about CDH. Is it true that there's some sort of treatment you can do on CDH babies in utero that can help improve their outcomes?"

"Ah, yes," she said. "You're referring to FETO, or fetoscopic endoluminal tracheal occlusion. It's a procedure that can be done on fetuses with severe cases of CDH to promote the growth of their lungs and improve survival outcomes. It involves blocking the trachea, which causes fluid to build up in the fetus's lungs. This fluid buildup stimulates lung growth.

"Unfortunately," she added, "FETO has proven to be too risky to perform on a pregnancy with twins. I'm sorry, but I'm afraid we won't be able to offer it."

Mau and I exchanged a disappointed look.

"We're very sorry to hear that," I said.

Dr. Blair pressed on: "I'd like to arrange a few appointments for you. We'll send you over to the children's hospital to speak with a surgeon who will explain a little bit more about the surgery, treatment, and recovery. We'd also like you to have a fetal MRI, which will allow our team to evaluate the organs involved and calculate lung volumes, and a fetal echocardiogram to evaluate heart structure and function. These tests will give us information about how the baby could be impacted after birth. In addition, we'll arrange for you to receive genetic counseling. Our office will contact you with the appointment information."

With one last sympathetic smile from the doctor, our appointment was over. Still in a daze, we somehow managed to make our way back to the waiting room.

The day hadn't gone the way I'd expected. At all. From assuming my child was relatively fine to discovering the severity of his condition to being counseled to abort to being compelled to meet with a surgeon—it was an onslaught of information and emotion. I noticed the other pregnant women and their partners waiting to be called back. I wondered what challenges they were facing, what fears they harbored. Had their hopes been crushed too?

As we looked at the ultrasound photos of our little boy and girl, it was difficult to believe that anything could be amiss. Over the past several weeks I'd been decorating the twins' room, and I knew these images would be displayed with pride in the new frames I'd recently purchased.

I'd already found matching cribs and sheets, choosing colors that felt calm and soothing. Now I wondered if that room would hold just one baby instead of two. I wondered if our baby boy would get the lifesaving surgery he so desperately required. I wondered what the future might hold for him, for our family. Was the Lord with us in this storm? Had He deserted us, or was there somehow a plan in all this?

I wondered.

CHAPTER 4

IN WHOM DO I TRUST?

"Before I formed you in the womb I knew you,
and before you were born I consecrated you."
JEREMIAH 1:5

Mau and I made our way back to the car in silence. I felt numb, unsure of what to say or do—detached from my emotions. The reality of the situation had yet to sink in.

Finally I turned to Mau. "So?" I asked. "How are you doing? What are you thinking?"

Mau's head was bowed. He looked up at me and took a deep breath as if to gather strength. Then, in his trademark strong and assured manner, measuring each word, he replied: "Well, I know that God's in control. He can do whatever He wants. God will heal this little guy one way or the other. He'll either heal him here on earth and let our baby come home with us or He'll heal him in the life to come if He decides to take our son to his heavenly home. I know it's easy to say that, but this is hard, so hard."

Mau paused. "How about you?" he asked. "How are you holding up?"

"I don't know what to think," I said. "This all feels so unreal. It's hard to believe this is happening, that our baby is actually that sick."

Mau took my hand, bowed his head, and prayed.

"Dear Lord, we thank You that You're always with us and You promise never to forsake us. Thank You that You go before us and You know what we need even before we ask. Please give us Your strength to make it through this ordeal, and please fill us with Your peace. We place this boy we cherish so much in Your hands, and we ask, if it be Your will, that You spare his life and let him live. We trust in You and know that You are a strong and powerful healer. Please also protect our little girl—we thank You for her precious life too. We ask that, whatever happens, people will see You at work and know that You are a good God."

I felt comforted in the moment, thankful that I wasn't alone in this darkness. We decided to grab coffee before picking up Thomas from a friend's house. As familiar landmarks passed by, I contemplated with sadness what the future might hold for our son. We pulled into the parking lot of a bustling donut shop, where the scent of sugary treats and fresh coffee attempted to raise our spirits. After collecting our drinks, we found a small table for two away from the doors. We had no desire to feel the chill each time they opened.

As I sat across from Mau, surrounded by tables filled with chatting people, sadness hit me like a massive wave. *Our son might die.* I didn't want it, I couldn't imagine it, yet it was a very real possibility. Just when we were prepared and eager to welcome *two* babies, would only one come home with us? *How could our joyous pregnancy have taken such a heartbreaking turn?*

My stomach felt like it was filled with a sack of lead. As I began to express my feelings to Mau, tears filled our eyes unbidden, streaming down our faces. Aware of the people around us, we managed to keep our anguish in check. We reminded ourselves that God was with us and would give us strength, but I couldn't will away the sinking feeling in my gut.

I felt comforted in the moment, thankful that I wasn't alone in this darkness.

We finished our coffee and picked up Thomas. On the way home I remembered that we were supposed to go to a friend's house for dinner. At first I thought we should still go, but as the afternoon wore on and my sorrow lingered, I realized I was in no condition to socialize. I called my friend and explained for the first time the heart-sickening news. As she expressed her understanding and support, I felt like I was watching someone else's life being played out on a screen. *This can't be happening to me, can it?*

But it was.

I also knew I needed to make another call. My parents knew we were going to the clinic for another ultrasound; they'd been praying and were surely waiting for an update. My mom answered the phone and called for my dad to join the conversation.

"So?" asked my mom cheerily. "How did it go?"

I could immediately tell that they, too, were hopeful—just as Mau and I had been—that the issue wouldn't be severe and might have even resolved itself.

"Well . . ." I hesitated. "Uh . . . the baby is not okay. It's actually quite serious." My voice cracked as I tried to hold back the tears; my body trembled. "The baby might not make it."

I collected myself enough to share some of the information we'd learned from the doctors, including their pressure to terminate the pregnancy.

"Oh, Christin, I'm so sorry," my mom replied. "This is not at all what we thought we'd hear."

"Yeah, I know . . ." Silence hung in the air, each of us not sure what to say.

My mom finally broke the stillness with reassurance. "Christin, we're here for you and Mau. We're going to pray, and we're going to ask God for a miracle. This isn't the end of the story, so don't give up, okay?"

"Okay, thanks, Mom," I replied, at least somewhat consoled. With hearts heavy and words spent, we said our goodbyes. Sitting nearby, Mau looked over at me with tenderness.

"I wonder if Mom and Dad will still move here?" I mused aloud, voicing one of the questions that had been lingering since arriving home that afternoon.

My mother and father were both raised in Edmonton, about three hours north of Calgary. Their roots run deep there. All their friends and most of their family members live in Edmonton. They love their home, their city, their church, and their family, yet my parents were considering relocating to Calgary.

It had all started almost a year earlier. Both my parents, though too young to retire, felt for different reasons that it was time for them to resign from their jobs, so in December 2015, after much prayer, they had. They had then sensed that the Lord was going to move them somewhere—not just to a different home but to a different city. They had no idea why or where, but they began to ready their house to sell while seeking the Lord's direction.

In August 2016 we learned that we were expecting twins, and Mau jokingly suggested they move to Calgary. That's when the idea had begun to percolate. Perhaps Calgary was where God was leading them?

My parents approached us in September and asked if we would want them to come. Of course we did, but we insisted that we wouldn't put any pressure on them; it had to be their decision. To leave their home, community, lifelong friendships, and two other children, they had to be sure. In October, after much prayer, my parents took a great leap of faith, put their house up for sale, and started looking for a new house in Calgary. Lord willing, they'd make the move sometime before the twins arrived.

At least that was the plan before we received this devastating diagnosis.

But now I wondered if they would come after all. *What if our baby boy doesn't survive and I have only one baby to care for? Maybe they shouldn't uproot their lives. Maybe we all misheard God.*

By February 2007 Mau and I had been spending a lot of time together, getting to know each other as friends to see if there was the potential for more. I'd never been in a serious relationship. I'd had no desire to waste my time with someone I didn't think I could marry, so while I'd had guy friends, my dating experience was limited. When we decided that we'd like to start dating, Mau felt it was important to ask my parents' permission to date me—a decision that would require a three-hour drive to Edmonton.

Although the conversation had the potential to be awkward, my parents and I both appreciated Mau's desire to honor them. The four of us met at a restaurant, the conversation flowed naturally, and Mau received their blessing. We began to date "officially," and it soon became obvious to both of us that this relationship could be headed toward marriage.

To show their support for Mau, my whole family—parents, older sister, and younger brother—traveled to Calgary later that year for a very special ceremony. At a government building downtown, Mau was sworn in as a proud new Canadian citizen.

By fall we were contemplating marriage, which meant a trip to Brazil so I could meet Mau's family over Christmas. I was not prepared for a city the size of São Paulo—the endless high-rises; the wide freeways; the maze of bumpy, narrow, house-lined streets; the lack of open space; and the vast number of people. In a place plagued with rampant crime, Mau's parents' house was built like a fortress: no yard, no front door, and no front windows. We entered the house through a locked garage door that led to not one but three separate doors, each with a distinct lock and key. Out back there was a high wall around the small courtyard, and each window was covered with bars. I couldn't go out on my own, and we had to speak English quietly so as not to draw attention to the fact that I was a foreigner.

Mau's family was very kind and welcoming, but I couldn't understand anything they said aside from the most basic Portuguese words. I sat silently through many extended family gatherings with a polite smile frozen on my face. The challenges of communication did not deter our relationship. Mau was a good host and even took me out for an all-you-can-eat Brazilian-style meal. I arrived back in Calgary hoping to marry this man.

+ + +

Mau's job with Promise Keepers Canada brought him to various churches all over western Canada to lead workshops, and every time he was invited to a church in the Edmonton area, Thomas and I tagged along to spend time with my family. This particular visit, however—the day after I broke the news to my parents—did nothing to lift my spirits from beneath a heavy cloud of sadness. I couldn't shake the fact that our once-joyous pregnancy story could end up a tragedy. The oppressive clouds refused to disperse all weekend.

After supper at my parents' house, once Thomas had gone to sleep, we sat in the living room with my parents. Our conversation inevitably turned to the babies and my parents' living situation.

"Have you guys thought about what you're going to do? Are you still planning to move to Calgary?" I inquired. They might not have made a final decision yet; still, I couldn't help but ask.

"Oh yes," replied my mom. "We've never changed our minds. We still feel that the Lord wants us there. If anything, we better understand now *why* He wants us to move. You're going to need even more support with a sick baby to care for than you would have otherwise."

In that moment I came to a profound realization. "God must love us an awful lot to send you to us," I said. My mom and dad laughed and nodded their heads.

I rejoiced with inward delight and an outward smile. I was very encouraged by their faith—they believed that our baby boy might survive! I could feel my own faith being bolstered as a result. To have not only their support but the gift of proximity and their regular presence in our lives was more than I had hoped for.

We returned home on Sunday evening, and the new week brought a shift in my thinking and my attitude. Mau and I committed to pray for our son's healing—not because we were sure it would happen, but because it was the only course of action we knew to take—moving forward in trust that God would let His perfect will be done. We were aware that the Lord may choose to take our son home to be with Him at birth, but we had nothing to lose and everything to gain by praying in faith.

As I read my Bible, a number of verses became anchors that I held to throughout the challenges we faced, especially when my fear attempted to overtake me. I realized more than ever before that the promises in God's Word are the sword that I can use to combat my fears.

Philippians 4:6-7 in particular came to my mind often: "Do not be anxious about anything, but in everything by prayer and supplication with thanksgiving let your requests be made known to God. And the peace of God, which surpasses all understanding, will guard your hearts and your minds in Christ Jesus."

Please save our baby boy became my daily prayer.

Another verse that I had memorized years ago played regularly in my mind: "Have I not commanded you? Be strong and courageous. Do not be frightened, and do not be dismayed, for the Lord your God is with you wherever you go" (Joshua 1:9).

I reminded myself often that, because God was with me on this difficult road, I didn't need to be afraid. Mau and I had taken up our shield of faith—a shield that deflected the devil's lies that we should abort our baby and doubt our God. We held tight to the sword of the Spirit, the Word of God, to counter the lies and move forward in battle against the enemy (see Ephesians 6:16-17).

I knew that I needed to take life one day at a time. As I read and meditated on God's Word, the Lord gave me an inexplicable sense of peace, just as He promises in Philippians 4:7. It was a profound and delightful sensation, like being cradled in strong, protective arms in the midst of a raging storm. That peace came from placing everything in the Lord's hands and letting go of what I couldn't control. It came from trusting the Lord with all my heart and not leaning on my own understanding, knowing that He would make my path straight (see Proverbs 3:5-6).

God had always been faithful to me. . . . I had to trust that He'd do so again.

So I continued to let those strong arms carry and comfort me, thankful that I didn't need all the answers and didn't need to know how the story would end. God had always been faithful to me, not by answering all my prayers the way I'd hoped he would but by providing comfort and guidance in the process. I had to trust that He'd do so again.

Now that we knew my parents were indeed coming to Calgary, Mau and I had two remaining priorities for prayer—that God would prolong my pregnancy until thirty-eight weeks and, of course, that He would save our preborn son.

Life soon returned to normal. Thomas and I resumed our daily activities, and I continued to search for baby supplies in duplicate for the twins' room. One day I was reminded of an artist I'd met who paints beautiful wall decor, and with immediate clarity I knew what I wanted for the babies' room—the colors, the look, and of greatest importance, the message. Within a few weeks, hanging on the wall were wooden boards painted aqua with white wording that read:

> For you *formed* my inward parts;
>   you *knitted me together* in my mother's womb.
> I praise you, for I am *fearfully* and *wonderfully* made.
> Wonderful are your works;
>   my soul knows it very well.

These verses—Psalm 139:13-14 with the italicizing added—were a declaration of our babies' design and worth. Both babies priceless, both loved, both having a purpose, both seen by their loving Father, and both deserving of our protection. God doesn't make mistakes. Though the clinic doctors would likely never see this artwork, it was my declaration to them that the child they viewed as disposable, whether he lived or died, was a beautiful creation of my God.

CHAPTER 5

A QUEST TO KNOW WHY

"Thus says the LORD: Do justice and righteousness, and deliver from the hand of the oppressor him who has been robbed. And do no wrong or violence to the resident alien, the fatherless, and the widow, nor shed innocent blood in this place."

JEREMIAH 22:3

Monday, November 21, 2016, was a big day. Less than two weeks after our life-changing appointment at the maternity clinic, Mau and I were on our way to meet with a surgeon at the children's hospital. I looked forward to learning about our son's treatment options and the surgery in particular—assuming the doctors approved it. The hospital was only about fifteen minutes from our home in light traffic, which I recognized as a blessing when I realized that in a few months' time we might be making this trek daily.

The hospital, which had only been open for ten years at the time, was sunlit, open, and inviting. The exterior of the building, with its red, blue, yellow, and green color palette, gave the appearance of a children's museum. As we entered, to our right we noticed kids playing in a center that offered free childcare for patients or siblings of patients. A wall of windows provided a spectacular westward view of the Rocky Mountains. This place didn't feel like a hospital—there were no poorly lit hallways, no pungent odors of chemical cleaners. Instead, the predominant aromas came from the coffee shop's dark brews and the cafeteria's hot comfort food. Vibrant children's artwork was visible up and down each corridor.

We'd arranged in advance to drop Thomas off at the day care, and we were pleased that he wasn't at all concerned about parting with us. We checked in at the surgery clinic and soon found ourselves shaking hands with a chipper surgeon who ushered us into a small room with a round table. The surgeon, Dr. Elder, looked to be in his midforties and appeared somewhat ruffled as he quickly acquainted himself with our file. His friendly manner put me at ease despite his seeming lack of preparedness.

Dr. Elder first showed us a diagram of a child with a left-sided hernia whose organs had moved up into the chest cavity. He realized at that moment that our son had a right-sided hernia, but he quickly pressed on and explained the difference between the two. Then he began to share the information we were most interested in hearing.

"As you've probably already been told," he said, "it's very important that your baby is not born early. We want his lungs to develop as much as possible before birth to increase his chances of survival, so in a best-case scenario, you'll be induced at thirty-eight weeks."

The children's hospital didn't have a maternity ward, so I learned that I'd give birth at a different hospital.

"After you've delivered your baby and he's been transferred to the children's hospital," Dr. Elder continued, "we'll need to wait until he's stable before we can proceed with the hernia repair. CDH babies are very sensitive to noise and movement, so the transfer by ambulance could be quite stressful."

When it came time for the surgery, he said, our baby would be given general anesthesia monitored by a pediatric anesthesiologist. The surgeon would make an incision just below the rib cage and guide the organs down into the abdomen. If there was enough muscle tissue, the hole in the diaphragm would be sewn closed, but if the hole was large, which was quite likely, they'd need to patch it.

We were surprised by what Dr. Elder said next: "The surgery—correcting the hernia—is the easy part." He looked over at me. "Even you could do it. If you've ever sewn fabric with a needle and thread, you could sew up the hole in the diaphragm."

Mau and I exchanged a grin. We doubted it was that simple, but who were we to argue?

Dr. Elder then turned to a picture depicting lungs and a heart. "The development of the lungs after the intestines and liver have been moved is of the upmost importance," he said. Some of this information we'd already learned, but a lot of it was new to us.

"The high pressure in the arteries makes the heart have to work harder than usual and can lead to heart failure. If the arteries close up, there's no way to open them up again. But there's no need to panic," he assured us with a smile. "The NICU team here will vigilantly monitor your baby's oxygen levels and will administer various medications to keep his arteries open and the blood flowing. Is this making sense?"

"More or less," we replied, although I was sure I wouldn't be able to remember all the details. What was clear, though, was that this surgery was merely the first step in our baby's journey. The continued development of his lungs would be a very delicate process requiring a team of highly trained professionals.

We knew the road ahead would be fraught with challenges, but I also heard an underlying message of hope. What a difference between this meeting with Dr. Elder and our meeting with Dr. Blair last week! Dr. Elder spoke of my child as a baby, not a fetus. He offered a potentially lifesaving treatment for my child, not more suggestions to end my child's life. He spoke of a process full of risk and uncertainty, yet he did so with an optimistic outlook. We welcomed this information and the hospital's willingness to try to save our baby's life.

Mau and I left encouraged, not knowing how much we would need this reinforcement in the days to come.

+ + +

The very next day we had an appointment with a geneticist back at the maternity clinic. The staff had arranged this meeting for us without much explanation, but I had an inkling of what was coming.

"You know that appointment we have tomorrow, honey?" I asked Mau. "The one with the geneticist? I think they're going to use it to try to convince us to have an abortion again."

"You think so?" Mau asked. "No . . . they wouldn't, would they?"

"Definitely," I said. "That's got to be the reason. I mean, I hope I'm wrong, but we'll find out soon enough."

I won't be caught off guard this time, I told myself, *and I won't be surprised by anything they spring on me.*

+ + +

The following day we sat down across from yet another doctor. He was soft-spoken and mild mannered with short salt-and-pepper hair. He was also dressed to impress.

The doctor began by detailing the genetic profile of our child. He explained that although the exact cause of CDH is unknown, it can be connected to a genetic condition or gene mutations. He said there's a chance that the fetus—our baby—would have other birth defects in addition to CDH.

I'd approached this appointment like a soldier on the lookout for threats, poised and ready to respond. I soon found myself shaking my head inwardly, both bemused and incredulous. The doctor had no specific information to offer because he had no genetic information from Mau, me, or the baby. *What's the point of this meeting? I don't need to know that my baby* might *have another issue—the doctor has no way of knowing anything with certainty. Is he trying to instill fear so that we'll want to have an abortion?* Let's just say I wasn't impressed.

He then took out a piece of paper and drew a line down the center. "Given this information," he said, pointing to one side of the line, "some couples might choose not to go forward with the pregnancy." He moved the pen to the other side of the paper. "Some couples, though, might choose to go forward."

His pen moved back and forth, drawing an invisible line that snaked its way down the page.

"It can be a difficult decision to make." Pause. "But you don't have long to decide." Pause. "We like to do the procedure by twenty-two weeks at the latest, and you're already twenty-one weeks along."

Anger filled me. I wasn't surprised by the turn of this monologue. My thoughts felt like a line of falling dominoes. Though he wasn't pushy, I was still upset that this doctor had even suggested this "procedure." I was angry that he proposed it in such a silky, seductive voice. I was angry that he didn't have the backbone to even use the word *abortion* but instead used a euphemism to muddle the gruesome truth of what abortion really is. I was angry that there seemed to be no one in this clinic willing to speak up for my baby. I was angry that my country has no laws to protect vulnerable preborn babies. I was angry that we had even been placed in this position. And I was angry with myself for not being able to voice my thoughts.

Anger filled me. . . . My thoughts felt like a line of falling dominoes.

Mau came to my rescue. He broke the silence with his direct, unflinching words: "You're talking about abortion," he said. "Out of curiosity, how would you terminate the baby, and what would happen to our twin baby girl?"

In my mind I gave my husband an imaginary high five.

I'm sure I grimaced as the doctor, who remained chillingly composed, described how they would stop our baby boy's heart and how I would somehow deliver our dead child. The hope, he said, was that our baby girl would survive, although there was a great risk of losing her as well. I felt sick to my stomach.

Mau nodded and replied with equal calm, "Well, thank you for explaining that to us. We won't be having an abortion. We're going to fight for both of our children's lives."

The doctor glanced at the frown etched on my face. "I had a feeling that's the direction you would take," he replied. "Before we wrap up, though, I should ask if you'd be interested in having genetic testing done on Twin A?"

"What would be the purpose?" I asked.

"To find out if he does, in fact, have any genetic defects."

"Will that affect my pregnancy or his treatment in any way?"

"No," he said, "it shouldn't affect treatment at birth. It would be for informative purposes."

"Well, in that case, no thank you."

I had no fear whatsoever about genetic defects, but it didn't really matter. We remained resolute. Nothing would sway Mau or me—our son would be born. If he did, in fact, have an additional birth defect, we would discover it at birth and address it accordingly.

In the days that followed, as I recalled our meetings with Dr. Blair and the geneticist, my mind replayed those conversations over and over again. As I did, a deep disquiet filled my thoughts. *Why? Why do so many people in our society think that aborting imperfect babies—or any babies, for that matter—is okay? Why do the doctors so freely offer abortion as a solution? Why don't they offer support or even just a glimmer of hope instead? Why do they use so many euphemisms for killing preborn babies:* reduction, termination, procedure*? Why have they never once used the word* abortion*? Why is there such a veil of secrecy? Why can't the babies just be born? Why do we have to abort them? Why, why, why?*

In my mind I gave my husband an imaginary high five.

As I pondered these questions, a profound sorrow began to grow within me. I realized that many other couples in our position would have chosen abortion. Faced with a devastating diagnosis and virtually zero encouragement to choose life, not to mention a medical professional's gentle suggestion to remove the "problem," it's no wonder plenty of parents give in. *How desperate and fearful they must be.* Without a firm foundational belief in the value of all preborn children, how easy it would be to be swayed in one's thinking.

Why do the doctors so freely offer abortion as a solution? Why don't they offer support or even just a glimmer of hope instead?

I certainly didn't know it at the time, but two years later I'd be diagnosed with cancer. I'd discover something in my arm, and the doctor would call the tumor what it was—a tumor. No discussion as to how I might choose to keep it or remove it. No euphemisms. Why? Because the clump of cells in my arm was just that—a clump of cells, ones that must be removed or I would die.

If a tumor is cancerous, left untouched it will grow, spread, and eventually kill. Therefore, the tumor must be removed. There is no tiptoeing around the issue. Remove it or die. But a pregnancy is different. A pregnancy is a new human life. Except in extremely rare circumstances, a pregnancy is not a death sentence the way cancer is. Abortion is the ending of a life, and that's why euphemisms are common—they attempt to gloss over the disturbing truth: The result of a successful abortion is a dead baby.

Why won't these doctors respect our decision to choose life for our son? It would seem that they weren't actually pro-choice but in reality pro-abortion. Though our culture endlessly repeats the phrase *My body, my choice*, I realized that these words didn't apply to us because *our* choice—the choice that Mau and I had made—ran counter to this mindset. Our culture routinely discriminates against unborn babies when prenatal testing indicates they *might* have a physical or intellectual disability. Rather than demonstrating true compassion by providing the care these babies need, the medical establishment often advocates for the false compassion that suggests ending precious lives before they're born—a permanent and tragically false solution.

If only parents who receive a prenatal diagnosis were given other options. If only they were offered hope. If only they knew that abortion wouldn't provide the peace or closure they desperately want. I've since learned that parents who choose to carry their babies to term, even after receiving a life-limiting diagnosis, report much lower rates of emotional distress (such as despair, regret, depression, and complicated grief) than those who don't.[1] These couples shower their babies with love, whether for minutes or months, until each one takes his or her final breath. I wish all expectant parents were provided with a more complete picture before making a choice with such massive ramifications.

Abortion is the ending of a life, and that's why euphemisms are common—they attempt to gloss over the disturbing truth: The result of a successful abortion is a dead baby.

To those parents who have already faced such a heartbreaking situation and have chosen abortion in response to a prenatal diagnosis, I would like to share the words of Laura Huene, founder of String of Pearls (stringofpearlsonline.org), an organization that supports families seeking to navigate their pregnancies and honor the lives of their babies when those babies aren't expected to live:

> [You] made the best decision [you] knew how to make with the information [you] had been given. There is no shame, there is healing available to [you] in the midst of [your] heartache. There is such grace and mercy for [you].[2]

God is here, ready to forgive you, longing to embrace you, desiring to heal you. Listen to these words from Psalm 103:8-12—they are true for everyone, including you, no matter the choices you have made:

> The LORD is merciful and gracious,
> slow to anger and abounding in steadfast love.
> He will not always chide,
> nor will he keep his anger forever.
> He does not deal with us according to our sins,
> nor repay us according to our iniquities.
> For as high as the heavens are above the earth,
> so great is his steadfast love toward those who fear him;
> as far as the east is from the west,
> so far does he remove our transgressions from us.

+ + +

These thoughts remained with me, percolating. My heart was hurting for other families and babies affected by life-threatening prenatal diagnoses, by biased and incomplete medical counseling, and by abortion itself. I was still in the middle of my own journey with this, but a passion for righting this injustice had been kindled.

CHAPTER 6

WORDS AND NAMES HAVE MEANING

But now thus says the L*ORD*,
he who created you, O Jacob,
he who formed you, O Israel:
"Fear not, for I have redeemed you;
I have called you by name, you are mine."
ISAIAH 43:1

Life carried us forward like a river's ceaseless flow. As a mom of a preschooler, I continued taking Thomas to playgroups, preschool, and swimming lessons. By the end of November, though I was only halfway through my pregnancy, I was already feeling uncomfortably large and lumbering. But Thomas was an active boy, so I managed as best as I could to keep up with him.

I soon discovered that even a quick Black Friday shopping trip was a lot to handle. I loaded Thomas into the car and made the five-minute drive to the mall. It was a chilly day, but nothing we couldn't manage.

Of course the parking lot was more packed than I'd ever seen. I drove around looking for a space but soon realized that it would be next to impossible to find one. I ended up parking a couple of blocks away on a side street—on the opposite side of the mall from the one store I wanted to visit. During my pregnancy with Thomas I'd felt strong and energetic throughout and had regularly gone on long walks right up until giving birth. So I figured visiting just one store should be a piece of cake, despite my current state. But I forgot several key pieces of information: I was pregnant with twins, Thomas could be trying at times, and I had to care for him alone on this outing. I didn't realize my mistake until it was too late.

We followed the sidewalk to the mall. Once inside, we looked in store windows along the way to our destination. Thomas was buckled in the stroller while I was trying to avoid the throngs of like-minded bargain hunters. By the time we finally reached our intended store, I was already beat, but I was also determined. I made some purchases, but now I was as exhausted as if I'd run a marathon. When I felt some cramping, I started to get worried. I didn't know if I had the strength to walk all the way back to the car.

Why didn't I just turn the car around and go home? Why, oh, why did I have to park so far away? My first thought was to call Mau, but he was out of town for work. I tried to think of someone else I could call to pick us up, but I didn't want to put anyone out. That left me with one choice: Make it back to the car one way or another.

"Hey, buddy, Mommy needs to sit down for a rest," I told Thomas. "Here we go. This looks like a nice bench. How about we have a snack and some water and take a look around?"

I handed Thomas a granola bar, thankful for a chance to regain some energy for the return journey. When we set out again, I moved at a snail's pace, the pain and cramping a great cause for concern.

Lord, please help me do this, I prayed as I willed myself to keep moving. *I feel so weak—I'm scared, Lord. Please keep the babies safe and help Thomas cooperate.*

We took breaks every so often as I shuffled along with caution, pushing the stroller and wishing I could hold my belly for support. I thanked God that Thomas was in a good mood. We left the warmth of the mall and at long last made it back to the car. Driving home I chided myself for being so foolish. *All for a bagful of clothes. I've learned my lesson and will be careful to respect my physical limitations. I can't afford to make that mistake again.*

Lord, please help me do this, *I prayed as I willed myself to keep moving.*

+ + +

In December I began the first of many regular visits to the maternity clinic. My appointment began with an ultrasound to take measurements of our baby boy's lungs, to track the overall development of both babies, and to measure the amniotic fluid surrounding them. After the ultrasound, a nurse checked my blood pressure and weight and then asked me questions about my health. Satisfied, she left me to wait for the doctor.

In the Canadian healthcare system, when a doctor refers their patient to a specialist, the patient typically has no say as to whom they will see. When I was pregnant with Thomas and knew I would arrive home from Brazil later in my pregnancy, I was fortunate that my cousin, who works as a pharmacist in the hospital where I gave birth to Thomas, was able to help refer me to an obstetrician with whom she worked. This time, however, I had no choice but to go to this clinic. It was run by a team of doctors who randomly rotated through the patients, so I never knew who I'd see and never had an opportunity to develop any sort of rapport with anyone.

By this point in my experience with the clinic, I should have known to prepare myself for some sort of distressing encounter, but my guard was down, thinking we had already resolved the matter of our choice. I was wrong.

A no-nonsense doctor I'd never seen before came in. After a few preliminary questions, she asked, "So I see that you want to go ahead with your pregnancy. Are you sure you don't want to terminate?" She directed the question at me like an arrow to the heart. I detected no warmth in this woman.

"Yes, I'm sure," I said.

"You do realize that we don't think your baby will survive."

"Well, I realize the severity of the situation. I understand the implications," I replied like a cowering child.

She looked at me with what seemed like thinly veiled contempt. "If you won't reconsider, then we'd suggest palliation."

"What is that exactly?" I asked.

"Basically, you would give birth to the baby and we would support you through the process of the baby's passing. It's an approach that helps relieve the suffering of the child and supports the family in the end-of-life process."

They want us to let him die at birth! They don't want to treat him. Oh, how I wish Mau were here to verbalize our wishes once more! He's so much stronger than me. I shriveled up inside but replied with simple conviction, unwilling to give in. "No," I said. "We want you to try to save his life."

I felt so exposed, even attacked—taken for a naïve fool for daring to choose life and hope. The doctor looked at me with cool disdain. Gone were the soft, compassionate words of previous doctors who had offered us a "choice"—replaced by unspoken scorn for what this doctor deemed to be our foolish beliefs. Hearing my answer, she told me to come back in two weeks for my next checkup and concluded the appointment with abrupt efficiency.

Gone were the soft, compassionate words of previous doctors who offered us a "choice"—replaced by unspoken scorn for what they deemed to be our foolish beliefs.

If I thought this was the last I'd hear about palliation, I was mistaken. The clinic suggested it again, not one but two more times! The trauma I'd already experienced by this point had tempered much of my anger, but after being blindsided yet again, I was frustrated that these doctors wouldn't respect our choice. *Isn't that what they say this is all about? Choice? The ability to choose what you'll do with your body, although there are actually two distinct human bodies involved? The ability to choose life or death. The ability to choose without coercion. Well, we've chosen life, so why can't they just stop pushing their agenda and leave us be?*

My thoughts didn't stop there, however. *Don't they realize that a prenatal diagnosis doesn't* guarantee *a postnatal prognosis? Have they never seen someone beat the odds?* Though they would likely never admit it, I wondered if some of this pressure stemmed from the fact that our son's NICU stay would cost our publicly funded healthcare system many thousands of dollars.[1]

+ + +

In the years since my pregnancy with the twins, I've learned about perinatal hospice, or perinatal palliative care. In essence, it involves creating a system of support for parents who choose to continue their pregnancies after receiving a prenatal diagnosis suggesting that their baby has a life-limiting condition and might die before or shortly after birth. This support continues from the time of diagnosis through the baby's birth and death. According to the website for Perinatal Hospice and Palliative Care, "Perinatal palliative care helps parents embrace whatever life their baby might be able to have, before and after birth."[2]

A distinctive aspect of this care model is the development of a birth plan that details the parents' wishes for everything from labor and delivery to how they'd like to spend their time with their baby (with options like photography, handprints or footprints, and allowing visitors). This includes plans for if the baby lives and if the baby passes away. With a plan in place, every moment is cherished, and parents can experience some solace by having a say in an otherwise devastating situation.[3]

On a *Revive Our Hearts* podcast episode, host Nancy DeMoss Wolgemuth interviewed a young mom, Kendal, who had given birth to a little girl who had been discovered in utero to have only half a heart. The mortality rate for this condition is high, and little Emery lived for just three months before she was taken off life support.

Kendal recounted:

> I remember them asking us if we were ready. I couldn't speak. I remember thinking, *No, no! How is anybody ever*

> *ready for this?* . . . All of her [life] support was taken off. I was just holding her. . . . Her head was where my heart is, and I was holding her, and [my husband] was holding me. We had thirty-two minutes of holding her before she passed away. But in that moment I felt Jesus's presence. I really felt like He was holding all three of us. . . . Even if I knew the final outcome, if I knew she was going to die in my arms, I would do it all again. I would do it again and again and again. It's just so worth it to be able to have any amount of time with your children, no matter how short.[4]

When my doctors recommended palliation, I have to wonder if my doctors were referring to perinatal hospice. Why didn't even one of them take the time to thoroughly explain it to us? Why wasn't perinatal hospice offered from our very first appointment? Why didn't anyone have the compassion to explain the concept to us? We wouldn't have changed our minds about trying to save our boy, but at least we'd have known that a life-honoring option was available.

By January I was thirty weeks pregnant, and two exciting events were approaching: my parents' move and my baby shower. My parents had sold their house in Edmonton and were moving into their new house in Calgary at the end of the month. Though their home wouldn't be in our neighborhood, a twenty-minute drive sure beat three hours, and their new place became our second home in no time.

Mau and I had been discussing names for the twins. One consideration was how a name sounded in both English and Portuguese. I wanted each name to sound similar no matter who was speaking it. Also, Brazilians like traditional names, so anything unusual or trendy by North American standards was a no-go. Remarkably, choosing our little girl's name was as easy as winter days are short. We quickly agreed on her first and middle names. But our little boy's name required much more deliberation. (We planned to wait until our twins were born to reveal their names.)

Mau and I both believe that names can have rich significance. The Bible is full of names that have meaning. For example, in the book of Matthew an angel appears to Joseph and tells him not to be afraid to take Mary as his wife, that she will have a son, and to "call his name Jesus, for he will save his people from their sins" (Matthew 1:21). Jesus' name, then, signifies His purpose. Because our little boy's right to life had been threatened, we decided that his name would be a declaration to the world of both his inherent worth and God's matchless power. After much research, thought, discussion, and prayer, we made our decision.

We have a supportive church community who had been following our pregnancy closely, so we decided to have a big baby shower right after church one Sunday. We invited everyone, and I was thrilled that my parents were there to celebrate with us. A friend with a gift for cooking and organizing parties took on the task of planning a Noah's Ark–themed shower. She'd apparently been waiting for the day when someone would be expecting boy-and-girl twins, and she went all out with the preparations! As people made their way to the downstairs fellowship hall, the room began to fill with happy chatter and smiling faces, not to mention a table overflowing with gift bags and lots of diapers.

Thomas was presented with a special gift said to be from his baby brother and sister—a tradition I've seen several times now at my Brazilian friends' baby showers. Being a musically inclined child, he seemed quite excited about his new glockenspiel.

Then Mau got up to speak.

"I want to thank you all for being here with us today to share in our excitement as we look forward to the arrival of our little ones. As you know, our little boy has been diagnosed with a life-threatening condition that affects the development of his lungs. Though the doctors have given us no hope, we know that God has promised to be with us and to walk with us," he said with feeling.

"The day before we received the news about our baby's condition, I was reading my Bible, and God gave me a beautiful promise from Isaiah 42:5-6. It says, 'Thus says God, the LORD, who created the heavens and stretched them out, who spread out the earth and what comes from it, who gives breath to the people on it and spirit to those who walk in it: "I am the LORD; I have called you in righteousness; I will take you by the hand and keep you."'

"It's God who gives us the breath and life we need to walk on this earth," Mau continued, "and it's God who will give breath and life to our baby boy if that's His will. Though we pray for our baby's healing, God's presence, character, and goodness are more important than the outcome."

Mau looked over at me with a sheepish smile and pressed on. "I wasn't going to do this, and I didn't talk to Christin about it. We were going to wait until the babies were born, but I'd like to share the twins' names with you.

"First is our little girl, who is so very precious to us. Her name is Emma Elizabeth. Emma means 'whole,' and Elizabeth means 'consecrated to God.' We pray she'll find lifelong wholeness in God and be consecrated to Him."

Mau paused for a moment. "Next is our little boy. His first name is Nathaniel, which means 'gift of God.' In a culture that deems his life worthless and disposable, we proclaim the opposite: He is beloved and priceless—he is a gift to our family. We accept him wholly and completely in the same way we welcome Emma, both beautifully and wonderfully made. His middle name is Joshua, which means 'the Lord is my salvation.'

"Not only is Nathaniel a gift from God, but we ask in faith that the Lord will save him physically. We serve a strong and powerful God, and we know that He is fully capable of saving Nathaniel if He chooses."

I actually didn't mind Mau sharing the babies' names. It felt appropriate for this event.

Mau continued, "Because we trust God, we ask everyone to pray for Nathaniel's healing, trusting that Jesus is going to answer that prayer—He's going to heal Nathaniel either by healing his physical body and sparing his life or by bringing him home. God is good, faithful, and loving, and we know we can rest in Him."

Our guests clapped in agreement as Mau took his seat. Two of our friends came over, knelt down beside us, and led the group in spontaneous prayer, petitioning the Lord to save our boy. It was a holy moment as God's people cried out to Him in faith. We could feel His presence as we prayed, "Lord, please save Nathaniel."

We could feel His presence as we prayed, "Lord, please save Nathaniel."

+ + +

A couple of weeks later, Mau came with me for my regular clinic appointment. This time I would see Dr. Blair, the head of the clinic. We hadn't met with her since that awful first appointment back in November.

Somehow the conversation steered to baby names. We told her that we had chosen the name Nathaniel for our son: *gift of God.* A declaration of his innate value and blessing to our family, no matter the state of his physical health.

We asked if she had any children. She did—a two-year-old boy. His name? Nathaniel. *Gift of God.*

Two boys from two different families. Two gifts of God. But we had to wonder if only one of them was a gift in the eyes of this doctor.

CHAPTER 7

THE FINAL LAP

My frame was not hidden from you,
when I was being made in secret,
intricately woven in the depths of the earth.
Your eyes saw my unformed substance;
in your book were written, every one of them,
the days that were formed for me,
when as yet there was none of them.

PSALM 139:15-16

As the weeks went by, God gave us continued peace and joy. My appointments at the clinic settled into a steady rhythm—ultrasound with a technician, checkup with a nurse, meeting with a doctor. The medical team finally accepted that we wanted lifesaving treatment for Nathaniel at birth, so they stopped suggesting palliation. Even better, they arranged for us to meet with a specialist from the NICU at the hospital that handled high-risk deliveries.

Mau joined me for this meeting as we took our now well-traveled route to the maternity clinic. Our city is one of the sunniest places in Canada, so even when the cold forces us inside our well-insulated buildings, we're still cheered by bright sunlight reflecting off the snow.

Dr. Evans sat across from us and began explaining, with a slight British accent, how we should expect the delivery of the babies to unfold.

"You're well on your way to reaching the thirty-eight-week mark," she said. "Continue taking care not to overexert yourself—we do not want these babies coming early." This was information we already knew quite well.

"Will I need to have a C-section?" I asked, hoping to avoid the procedure.

"If the babies continue to grow as well as they have been, we don't see an excess of amniotic fluid, and they're positioned properly for a vaginal delivery," she said, "then you shouldn't need one. We'd like to give you an epidural, though, just in case we need to perform an emergency C-section."

Dr. Evans described how I'd be induced and give birth with the NICU team in the room, ready to receive Nathaniel immediately after delivery. The team would include neonatologists, nurses, neonatal and surgical fellows, and respiratory therapists. Once Nathaniel was born, they'd fit him with a breathing tube connected to a ventilator to help him breathe.

"How are you both feeling about all this?" she asked.

"We're in a good place; we're at peace," Mau replied. "All we want is for your team not to withhold any resources. Please give your best, and we believe that God will do His part."

At the mention of God, the doctor shifted in her seat,

seemingly caught off guard. "Would you like me to shut the door?" she asked.

"No, we're okay," Mau replied without missing a beat. "We don't know what the outcome will be, but all we can ask is that you and your team do your best. And we're trusting that God will do whatever He decides is best."

The doctor nodded her head. "I hear you, and I appreciate where you're coming from. I can assure you that we'll do everything we can to save your baby. That's our job—we're in the business of saving babies, and everyone on the team is fully committed to providing the best care possible."

"Thank you, Dr. Evans," Mau said with a smile. "That's all we could hope or ask for. As we told the other doctors, we're fully aware of the implications of this diagnosis, and we're not in denial about what the outcome might be. We just want to give our son a chance to beat the odds and give God a chance to act."

We left the appointment encouraged, thankful to meet someone who was on our side and who wanted to help our son. We continued praying with expectancy for physical healing, but we prepared ourselves for a long, tough battle.

At this point I was counting down the days to my induction. My eagerness was perhaps heightened by the increasing unpleasantness of a womb growing ever outward. Simply washing dishes had become painful because my round belly extended so far out that I had to lean forward at an awkward angle to do them. I'd started wearing an elastic belt around my lower abdomen to support the weight and lessen the cramping. Many nights I was so hot and uncomfortable that even on cold winter nights when everyone else was bundled

We prepared ourselves for a long, tough battle.

up under thick comforters I ended up sleeping on the couch—the cool leather a refreshing reprieve for my overheated body. Most afternoons I was so tired that I put on a TV show for Thomas so I could rest. I felt guilty using the TV as a babysitter, but I was thankful to have the option.

By week thirty-six I was bursting with excitement—ready to meet our babies, ready for the next step of our journey, ready for the months of waiting and anticipation to end. I took a selfie in our bedroom mirror, a big smile on my face and a huge belly. I looked like I'd stuffed a beach ball under my sweater.

The ride was about to begin. The slow ascent—and the inevitable plunge—was imminent. I knew the ride would be full of harrowing dives, unpleasant bumps, sharp curves, and breakneck speeds. I knew I had no choice but to hang on, not knowing how it would all play out. I knew all this, and I was ready. That's because I also knew the One who was in control. I was confident that He knew each and every inch of this ride. He was the One who would keep me secure, who would protect me from falling. The One in whom I could trust. *Let's do this.*

The ride was about to begin. The slow ascent—and the inevitable plunge—was imminent.

+ + +

I was scheduled to be induced on Monday, March 20. On March 16 I went in for my last ultrasound. The doctor reported that the babies were continuing to do well and instructed me where I should go on Monday and what time to be at the hospital.

I can't believe I've almost made it! Just a few more days, and my babies will be born!

The morning of March 20 dawned bright and cool; the promise of new life and growth filled the air this first day of spring. Two overnight bags sat by the door—one for me and one for Thomas, who would be staying with my parents while I was in the hospital. The three of us ate breakfast at the kitchen table as I went through my mental checklist.

"Guess what, buddy?" Mau asked Thomas, his face beaming as he took a sip of coffee. "Today's a special day. Do you remember where you're going today?"

"Grandpa and Grandma's!" Thomas shouted with glee, always happy to go to his second home and see some of his favorite people.

"And where are Daddy and Mommy going?"

"To the hospital to have the babies!" he answered with shining eyes.

"That's right! Pretty soon you're going to see your new baby brother and baby sister. But first you get to sleep over at Grandpa and Grandma's house, and we'll see you tomorrow," Mau explained. Thomas skipped around the kitchen doing a happy dance in his pajamas.

We finished eating and prepared to leave. As I walked down the hall, I stopped to look in the babies' room. Everything was ready. Two cribs, a changing table, a rocking chair, and a diaper pail. Baby clothes, neatly folded and waiting for both boy and girl, all in their respective drawers. Diapers, blankets, books, stuffies—all there. We still had the white bassinet with the frilly cotton skirt that Thomas had slept in as an infant, and a new, narrow car seat for Thomas sat in the back of our car. We already had Emma's infant car seat, but I'd decided to wait and purchase Nathaniel's just before he was ready to come home from the hospital—the only thing that still remained on the list of items required for both babies.

Mau buckled Thomas in while I gingerly lowered myself with my large belly into the passenger seat. The cramping feelings that had followed me for weeks had not let up, but I barely noticed them now, less than an hour away from checking in at the hospital. My parents welcomed Thomas with big smiles and sent us on our way with a prayer, a hug, and the reassurance that we were not alone. The partially melted snow along the drive reminded us that spring had come and was starting to work its magic, freeing us from another long winter.

Mau looked over at me with concern and asked, "How are you feeling?"

I knew he was asking about more than just my physical well-being.

"I'm okay," I replied. "I'm ready. I just hope being induced is going to go all right. I wonder how long it's going to take and how everything will be." My words were vague, but I knew that Mau understood my tumult of thoughts and emotions.

For some reason I thought about the car seats. "I'm so glad we were able to find car seats to fit in the back. I didn't want to have to buy a new vehicle."

"Yes, me too," Mau replied. He took a quick glance at the back seat, noticing only two car seats—Thomas's and Emma's. "What did you end up doing? Did you buy car seats for both babies?"

"I just bought the one for the time being," I said. "I thought I could buy Nathaniel's later, when he's closer to coming home."

Mau nodded. "Ah, I see . . ."

+ + +

Like his twins soon to be born, Mau had his own harrowing birth story. I wonder how his mother, Odnea, must have felt when she went into labor with Mau three months early back in 1974. After giving birth to Mau's older brother, Odnea had experienced two miscarriages before conceiving Mau. How she longed to have another child! I can only imagine the fear she must have felt knowing that he was arriving too soon at a time when care for premature babies was very limited. The modern medical technology and highly trained NICU teams we now take for granted weren't available at that time in Brazil.

Mau was born in May, just as the cool winter months descended on São Paulo. Tiny Mauricio survived his birth, of course, but with no NICU for him, he was sent home under the vigilant care of his parents. Keeping their newborn warm was crucial, so they made him a makeshift incubator out of a wooden box and a heat lamp to ward off the cold in a concrete house constructed to keep out heat during the hot summer months. Full of faith, Odnea prayed that her son would survive, and survive he did. Little by little, day by day, Mauricio grew into a healthy, energetic little boy. Mau's mother will still tell you that he is a miracle child and that God has always had a purpose for his life.

+ + +

"Good morning," I greeted the woman sitting behind the desk at the maternity ward. I gave her my name and handed her my healthcare card. "I was told to come in today to be induced."

I changed into a hospital gown before being led to a long room with multiple beds. A nurse directed me to a bed, and Mau pulled up a chair while we waited for a doctor to examine me.

Once the doctor arrived, he explained that if I hadn't yet begun to dilate, they'd need to initiate a procedure to cause my cervix to soften and open. The process usually took about twenty-four hours, he said, so I might need to return to the hospital the next morning and would likely give birth the same day. Mau and I felt immediate disappointment—we were both geared up to have the babies as soon as possible.

"That being said," the doctor continued, "let's take a look, and then we'll decide on the best course of action."

He proceeded with the exam. "Good news, Christin. You're already four centimeters dilated, which means we should be able to proceed with the induction today."

Mau and I were beaming.

"We didn't expect you to be ready to give birth today," the doctor said, "so I'll need to make sure we have everyone assembled for the delivery. Assuming we do proceed, we'll admit you to a room and give you an epidural as a precaution in case you should require a C-section. Then we'll administer oxytocin intravenously, which will cause your uterus to contract. Now, if you don't mind, please wait here while our team discusses our course of action."

It wasn't long before the doctor returned with a smile. "Okay, we're all set. We'd like you to come back at one o'clock so we can begin inducing you today. We'll get your room ready, and in the meantime, you can enjoy a coffee or a bite to eat."

"Thank you so much," I said, exchanging a smile with Mau. I changed into my own clothes, and Mau and I headed down to the lobby.

"Where would you like to go?" Mau asked as he checked the time. "It's eleven o'clock, so we've got two hours."

"I guess we could get something for lunch," I suggested.

"You know," Mau said with a thoughtful expression, "I've been thinking about that car seat. I think we should go buy the second car seat right now."

"Sure," I replied after a pause. My mind immediately jumped to considering the logistics. "Do you think we have time? We only have a couple of hours. Which store should we go to? Maybe we should go to one near home so we can drop it off on the way back to the hospital. What do you think?"

"Sounds good to me," he said. "We'd better get going, then, if we want to make it back in time. Hopefully we'll have time for lunch, too."

We embarked on what had quickly become a very important mission. When I had decided not to buy the second car seat until later, it wasn't because I had consciously doubted that our baby boy would survive. Perhaps, though, deep down, a part of me wondered if I had better wait to save myself the heartbreak of having to return it later. Yet at that moment there was nothing more imperative than securing it as a symbol of our hope that the Lord would save Nathaniel.

We left the store with a large brown box squeezed into the back. We headed home to drop off the seat, found something to eat, and arrived back at the hospital right on time. We were filled with a sense of satisfaction. Mission accomplished.

Back in the maternity ward, my nurse, Jenny, directed me to a bed and got me started on oxytocin. The contractions started slowly at first but soon grew in intensity. A couple of hours later it was time for the epidural, after which I didn't feel much of anything. Goodbye, pain.

The room was quiet as Mau and I passed the hours reading—Mau on his phone and me a book. By nine thirty that night, Jenny determined that I was fully dilated. It was time to alert the delivery and NICU teams. The countdown was finally over. It was time to have these babies.

PART TWO

Birth and Beyond

CHAPTER 8

WELCOME TO THE WORLD, LITTLE ONES

Upon you I have leaned from before my birth;
you are he who took me from my mother's womb.
My praise is continually of you.
PSALM 71:6

I'm surrounded by doctors, OR nurses, and the NICU team. Bright white lights shine down on me, and I continue pushing with all my might.

"Great job! Keep going—we can see his head!" Dr. Sharma says.

The room is charged with anticipation, everyone poised like runners at the starting line ready to spring into action at the sound of the starter's gun.

The contraction ends, and another almost immediately begins. I push like I've never pushed before. Though I hardly feel a thing, I must be doing something right because Dr. Sharma exclaims, "That's it. That's it! Here he comes!"

I glance down to see Dr. Connor ready to catch my baby in his hands, Dr. Sharma at his side.

I know the moment Nathaniel is born. I hear his cry. One strong cry—a breathtaking sound—that lasts but a second as the final bit of oxygen I can provide him is used up. That cry is followed by silence. His battle to survive has begun.

The doctors quickly pass Nathaniel to the NICU team. A nurse notes the standard information: born March 20, 2017, at 10:02 p.m. Birth weight: six pounds, three ounces, or about 2.8 kilograms. Mau, who has been at my side the whole time, is now on the other side of the room, watching Nathaniel as the team intubates him and connects multiple sensors to his little body. They deftly insert the breathing tube in a matter of seconds, the respiratory therapist ensuring that Nathaniel receives the proper amount of oxygen to stabilize. Since I can see nothing but the backs of five or more hospital staff members, I turn my focus back to the task at hand: delivering my little girl.

I know the moment Nathaniel is born. . . . His battle to survive has begun.

I have to trust that the professionals in blue scrubs know what they're doing. I look to my right, wishing that Mau were back at my side. He is actually on his phone, punching out a message that I can only assume is an update to everyone that Nathaniel has been born and is successfully intubated. Though that message can wait, I try to be understanding because I know he's overwhelmed and has been, in his own words, "so focused on making sure that everything's okay with Nathaniel."

My thoughts are interrupted by Dr. Sharma's voice. "All right,

Christin. I need a big push from you. That's it. Keep going. Here she comes! Keep pushing!"

I make one giant, final push. Mau makes it back to my side just in time as baby Emma is born. Unlike Nathaniel, she doesn't make any sound at first. The seconds tick by, each one an eternity, until her cry comes forth like bells on Christmas morning. The nurses clean her up, weigh her, and place a cream-colored cap on her head. With great delight I welcome her into my embrace for some skin-to-skin bonding time. As Mau looks on in wonder, I marvel at the beauty of new life, gazing at her chubby pink cheeks, eyelids clamped shut, and delicate little fingers. I'm told that her time of birth is 10:13 p.m., her birth weight six pounds, eleven ounces, or 3.04 kilograms. The room still bustles with activity, but for the moment my eyes are fixed on this little one.

+ + +

By ten fifty, the doctors and nurses caring for Nathaniel have been working on him nonstop, with Mau by his side watching the proceedings. One of the nurses tells Mau, "You can take a couple of pictures now before we wheel him to the NICU."

"Thank you," Mau replies as he pulls out his phone.

Nathaniel is on his back, wearing a newborn diaper and nestled in multiple blankets. He's quite pink except for his purple fingers and is covered all over in patches of a white, filmy substance. He wears a cap identical to Emma's and has dark hair peeking out from underneath (Mau says he saw a full head of hair).

Not only is there a breathing tube for his mouth, but another tube keeps Nathaniel's stomach decompressed to assist his lungs.

Sensors attached to his chest track his heart rate and function, and additional tubes inserted into his umbilical cord monitor blood levels and administer medication. And if that weren't enough, he has a sensor attached to his right foot and yet another to his right hand. At least nine lines and tubes extend from Nathaniel's body—each a life-giving appendage of sorts that administers oxygen and medication, tracks vitals, or sounds an alarm when a reading is too high or low.

Despite all this technology designed to support and comfort him, our baby boy does not lie in silent slumber, blissfully unaware of his circumstances. (How I wish that were so, but no.) With herculean effort Nathaniel takes each laborious breath, his stomach and chest heaving in and up in an unnatural, shuddering motion. Pain and anguish are etched on his face, his mouth open in a silent, heart-wrenching cry, his eyes closed beneath his deeply furrowed brow. How we wish we could shield him from this hardship, but there's nothing we can do but be with him and pray. *Lord, help him breathe. Please keep him stable. Keep him safe. Guide the doctors and nurses caring for him. Please save him. Please, O Lord, please.*

Pain and anguish are etched on Nathaniel's face, his mouth open in a silent, heart-wrenching cry.

This is just the beginning of the struggle, yet so far Nathaniel is strong. The Lord is with him and is already answering prayer. For the first time we hear the words we crave: *better than expected.* The doctor says, "The intubation went better than expected." Our hearts rejoice. *Thank You, Lord! Thank You for hearing our prayers, and thank You for Nathaniel's life. Please continue to protect him.*

+ + +

How different this day could have been if the doctors hadn't agreed to treat him. Nathaniel would be in my arms, eyes closed, likely never to open. Rather than looking at tubes and an Isolette, I would be gazing at his sweet face with a mixture of love and heartbreak. Rather than having a room filled with medical staff, we would be surrounded by family. Rather than anxious butterflies and whispered prayers, tears would cascade down from overflowing fountains of grief. We would take photos to forever capture these fleeting, precious moments. Thomas would kiss his baby sister's and baby brother's soft heads, perhaps unaware that he would never see his brother again. Emma would then be lovingly passed from one family member to the next with misty eyes and smiles of adoration. We would shower a lifetime of love on Nathaniel before finally letting him go.

The mere thought of this alternate reality wrecks me. Why were we so fortunate as to be given a chance? I don't know. We'd done nothing to deserve it. I'm incredibly thankful that my baby is receiving lifesaving care, but my heart aches for those who've lost a child while my own has just begun his fight for life.

+ + +

Mau and I watch as Nathaniel is wheeled out of the OR. He's on his way to the NICU, just a short walk down the hallway. Emma and I, with Mau at our side, are taken to a vacant room for two in the maternity ward. A nurse comes in to help me breastfeed Emma, and I convince her that Emma will probably need to be supplemented. I learned the hard way after having Thomas that I can't produce enough milk and have no choice but to top off the meal with formula after each feed. Once Mau ensures that we're settled in, he makes his first visit to the NICU to spend some time at Nathaniel's side. I'm in no condition yet to make that trip, so Emma and I enjoy a few hours of sleep before her next feeding.

The next morning dawns overcast with the threat of snow. Another patient has moved in next to me, and the curtain is drawn to give us the semblance of privacy. A doctor checks on Emma and me and determines that we're both in good health.

I feel content with Emma by my side, but I'm anxious to know how Nathaniel is doing and even more anxious to see him. Mau speaks with Nathaniel's neonatologist and learns that during the night Nathaniel's carbon dioxide (CO_2) levels were very high, which means he wasn't responding to the ventilation machine as hoped. This is a concern because he needs to be stable before being transferred to the children's hospital. Once there, they'll be able to continue his treatment and perform the surgery to repair his diaphragm. The news gets worse as the doctor explains that they can't transfer Nathaniel on the current machine. His CO_2 levels must come down and his lungs must be able to tolerate the original equipment. They hope to transfer him in the next thirty-six hours, which means his condition needs to improve a lot in a short period of time.

Absorbing this news, Mau immediately sends out the first of many updates that will bring together family, friends, and friends of friends across Canada and Brazil to pray for miracles one step at a time.

We take this information in stride. Mau alternates between reading his Bible, bonding with Emma in my room, and spending time in prayer at Nathaniel's bedside in the NICU. By early afternoon Emma is beside me in a little bassinet on wheels, wrapped snuggly in a hospital-issue flannel blanket. Her dark, languid eyes blink as Mau croons over her in Portuguese. My parents and Thomas enter the room to meet one of the new additions to our family.

"Hey, Thomas!" we exclaim. "How are you, buddy? We've missed you!"

"Good!" says Thomas, dressed in his favorite gray and fluorescent orange T. rex shirt.

"Do you want to meet your little sister? This is Emma." I motion to the little bundle Mau has placed in my arms.

Thomas walks over with a shy smile and plants a sweet little kiss on his sister.

My parents have brought gifts—a beautiful hand-knit pink cap for Emma, a matching blue cap for Nathaniel, and a colorful bouquet for me.

"We found these caps at a Christmas market. It was after we found out about Nathaniel's diagnosis, but we bought one for him in faith."

"Thank you," I reply. "I love them!" I replace the drab cap Emma's been wearing with her new one. "I'll keep Nathaniel's close by so it's here when he's ready."

My parents each take a turn holding their new granddaughter, but they're also eager to meet Nathaniel, so Thomas stays with Emma and me as Mau leads them to the NICU. They scrub up to enter the dark, quiet corner where he lies in his Isolette. As much as I long to see him too, I'm still working up the strength to walk over. I know my turn is coming soon.

"He has very delicate features," my mom tells me when they return. "And a head of dark hair. He's very beautiful."

I smile and nod, but I'm struck by how strange and depressing it is that I haven't seen my son with my own eyes yet. I'm thankful, though, that my parents have seen little Nathaniel.

As our visit draws to an end, Mau and I give Thomas a big hug.

"Bye, dude. Love you so much!" I say with a grin.

"We miss you, buddy," Mau says, "but Mommy and Emma are coming home from the hospital tomorrow. So we'll see you soon, okay?"

"Okay," Thomas replies. "Bye, Daddy. Bye, Mommy." He gives Emma a little hug, and we thank my parents for taking good care of Thomas. It comforts us to know that he's in good hands and is so comfortable with his grandparents.

After they leave, I decide I'm ready to visit the NICU. We're directed to leave Emma in the nursery, so I cautiously bring my legs over the edge of the bed and stand up. My body is still racked with pain, the epidural long worn off. Mau carries Emma while I hobble at his side, making our way into the nursery, where a couple of other babies rest in bassinets. With Emma safely deposited, I link arms with Mau and continue the interminable journey down a hallway that seems to stretch on for miles. The pain compels me to take just one tiny step after another. With a sigh of relief, I sink into a chair halfway down the hall for a much-needed break.

I'm struck by how strange and depressing it is that I haven't seen my son with my own eyes yet.

After what seems like an eternity, we arrive at the NICU desk. Only the parents or guests in the company of the parents are allowed to visit the baby.

"Hi, we're here to see Nathaniel Rosa," Mau informs the unit clerk, who nods with a smile of recognition. He opens a red binder and shows me where to sign in. We then scrub with soap up to our elbows for a full thirty seconds. We find Nathaniel's Isolette in the remotest back corner, away from much of the hustle and bustle of the NICU. Every inch of his Isolette is covered by a special blanket. There's a monitor at the head of the bed along with six smaller devices with blue screens and buttons. At the foot of his bed several plastic tubes connect to the ventilation machine that pushes oxygen into his lungs. I know nothing of the intricacies involved or what each screen and device tracks; I'm just thankful he's alive.

Nathaniel's nurse comes over and speaks to us in a hushed tone. She removes the blanket so we can look at him, but he's much too unstable for us to touch him. Though his face is visible, I can barely make out his features in the dim light. Nathaniel lies still, eyes closed and mouth open with two tubes coming out, no longer struggling to breathe like he was the night before. Though he appears to rest in peaceful slumber, the tubes attached to his body are definitely not comforting. A look at the monitor reveals that his oxygen saturation and blood pressure levels are both low. I don't realize the significance of those numbers and will continue to remain quite ignorant. This ignorance, I later conclude, is actually a blessing that shields me from carrying an even greater burden.

I'm overcome with gratitude that Nathaniel has survived the first step of his monumental battle. As a very pragmatic person, I'm not filled with uncontrollable grief to see him in this state, nor am I reduced to tears because I can't hold him. I know he's exactly where he needs to be. I am sad, however, that I don't know what he looks like and wonder how long it'll be until I can properly look at his little face.

I try to ignore the pain radiating up and down my back. I want to be with my little boy, but after five minutes I can no longer bear it and must find a seat. Mau and I soon begin the uncomfortable walk back to the maternity ward.

Mau later returns to the NICU to gain a better understanding of our son's situation. He knows that in order to transfer Nathaniel to the children's hospital, which the doctors would like to do tomorrow, he needs to stabilize first. Unfortunately, his carbon dioxide (CO_2) and oxygen (O_2) levels, his blood pressure, and his lung pressure are all still oscillating. And because Nathaniel's lungs are so underdeveloped, they've had to put him on a high-pressure ventilator.

Before moving on to the next patient, the doctor says, "Nathaniel's feisty. He's fragile but a warrior."

Armed with this new information and filled with hope, Mau sends out the next prayer update. Our requests are that Nathaniel's blood pressure will stabilize, his oxygenation will improve, he'll be less agitated, and he'll be transferred to the children's hospital tomorrow.

Later in the day, Mau learns that Nathaniel's numbers have balanced out, and assuming the numbers remain optimal, he'll be moved to a lower-intensity ventilator in the morning. All he'll need at that point is a short window wherein he's stable enough to be transported.

God is answering our prayers already, but questions fill my head as Mau relays the news. *Will Nathaniel stabilize enough to make the trip to the children's hospital? What will tomorrow bring?*

CHAPTER 9

A VERY PRESENT HELP IN TROUBLE

"Where two or three are gathered in my name, there am I among them."

MATTHEW 18:20

By our second morning at the hospital, Emma and I are preparing to be discharged. My time with Emma has been very special, and we're already forming an inseparable bond.

Mau walks into our room after spending the night at home. "Hey, honey. How did you two sleep?"

"Pretty good overall," I reply. "Emma was up every few hours to eat. So far she's been such a content baby. How about you?"

"Not bad. It was good to sleep in my own bed.

"So," he continues, "I just went to check on Nathaniel, and I was able to speak with the doctor. She said he did well; his numbers have remained stable, so they're still planning to transfer him today. The doctors are checking his heart now. This'll help them determine when to swap the machines and prepare for the transfer. But"—he frowns—"when I left the NICU, Nathaniel was requiring more oxygen from the machine than they'd like to see."

"Okay . . ." I reply with a mix of relief and alarm. "Why don't we pray; then I'd like to go see him again before we leave."

"Sounds good," Mau says. He takes my hand, and together we seek our loving Father, the One we trust to carry us through this storm. Mau also sends out another request asking our friends and family to pray. He closes the message with one of my favorite Scripture passages:

> "You keep him in perfect peace
> whose mind is stayed on you,
> because he trusts in you.
> Trust in the Lord forever,
> for the Lord God is an everlasting rock."
>
> ISAIAH 26:3-4

We arrive in the NICU just as the medical team has gathered to review Nathaniel's case. We join the circle of doctors, nurses, respiratory therapists, and pharmacists as they discuss his current condition and treatment plan. In general they're very satisfied with how things are going; they're just waiting for the result of an echocardiogram before proceeding. The team at the children's hospital has been following Nathaniel's case closely and has his room ready and waiting.

By late morning we've checked out of the hospital and all three of us are on our way to my parents' house. We plan to stay there for a few days while we make frequent trips to the hospital. Mau returns to the NICU that afternoon and is thrilled to see the medical team preparing for our boy's transfer. They've brought in special equipment for the move and tell Mau that the children's hospital will call when Nathaniel arrives. Just a few more hours!

At my parents' house Thomas plays with ceaseless energy and Emma takes turns snuggling with Grandma, Grandpa, and me. My body still aches and I'm exhausted, unable to do much more than take care of Emma's needs, so I'm grateful for the respite.

The situation I could only imagine months ago is now our life: trying to care for three children—one healthy newborn, one hospitalized newborn, and one spirited preschooler. I had plenty of help as I learned how to care for newborn Thomas, including the luxury of focusing all my energy on that task—no meals to cook, groceries to buy, house to clean, or older children to care for. I barely left the house the first month other than to take Thomas out in the stroller for pleasant summer strolls or to medical checkups. Unbeknownst to me at the time, it feels like God was allowing me to work out all my new-mom jitters and worries in a supportive environment in order to prepare me for this much greater challenge to come.

I can't just go home and recover for a week or so while I adapt to caring for the new additions to our family. My body doesn't get time to rest and heal. Daily trips to and from the hospital with a newborn and, at times, a preschooler in tow, are about to begin. Not only that, but no matter where I am I'm separated from one or more of my children. There's not a moment when I'm not torn. If I'm at home or at my parents' house meeting the needs of my two healthy children, I'm plagued

This inability to be everywhere at once, to be there for all my children, especially Nathaniel, is like an arrow to the heart.

with guilt that I'm not at the hospital with Nathaniel. But if I'm at the hospital with Nathaniel and Emma, it means that Thomas isn't with me.

This inability to be everywhere at once, to be there for *all* my children, especially Nathaniel, is like an arrow to the heart. And it's barely just begun. I can already feel it just two days into this journey. My child is at the hospital, all alone, fighting for his life, and I'm not there with him. *Lord, help me be strong! Help me be there for my family.*

I was a timid, studious child. Content with a few good friends and books to read, I avoided drawing too much attention to myself. Talking to strangers (or even family members I didn't know well) wasn't easy for me, and as I got older the concept of complete independence was intimidating. On a scale of one to ten, my self-confidence rated about a two, so I needed God to help me put my confidence in Him. As a teenager I began taking conscious steps to stretch my comfort zone. I (instead of my mother) started making my own appointments. I applied and interviewed for part-time jobs, and I volunteered at a long-term care home. These seemed like simple steps, but they were monumental things for a quiet girl like me.

At odds with my timid nature was my increasing desire to travel—to see the world beyond Canada. A missions trip to build a house in Mexico with my high school youth group was life-changing. I'll never forget the simple structure we built, little better than my family's garage back home, or the feeling of gratitude for my life of relative plenty.

The next time I left home I was nineteen and working toward a degree in education. I traveled to China for several weeks with a group of Bible college students to teach English. I strengthened my growing sense of independence by staying in the home of a host family and making my way with another girl to and from the school each day. The streets there vibrated with life. The aroma of grilled foods from street vendors mixed with the fumes of vehicles weaving their way through crowded roads. It was a cacophony of honks, unintelligible words, and Chinese music wafting from open storefronts.

That was the same year that Mau, at age twenty-seven, left hot and humid São Paulo for dry and sunny Calgary. He had done his own fair share of traveling and was excited to experience Canada. Arriving in August, he enjoyed the final warm days of summer and earned the worst sunburn of his life while rafting down a river. As his graduate studies in architecture began, the days soon cooled from the vibrant colors of autumn to those of the inevitable cold, dark winter.

No one prepared Mau for the frigid cold of an Albertan deep freeze, though to him it was just another new experience. When temperatures dip to thirty below zero, most Canadians spend as little time outdoors as possible. But not Mau. His brother happened to be visiting him at the time, so the two explorers bundled up to survey the empty downtown streets. Without the luxury of a car, Mau had already become accustomed to walking, biking, or taking the train everywhere, so why stop now? This was an adventure.

Yet Mau almost dropped out during his first semester. If he wasn't in a lecture, he was studying. Sunup to sundown, nothing but schoolwork. And all day every day, nothing but English. His head ached. His brain strained to understand the rapid speech, graduate-level language, and unfamiliar accents. His English was good, but this felt overwhelming.

"I think I should take a year off to improve my English," Mau said to his thesis supervisor. "I'm having a hard time keeping up."

His supervisor paused to consider. "I don't think that's such a good idea," he replied. "If you leave now, you might never come back. I think you can do it."

Mau decided to take his advice, and he never looked back. The library was his home for the next three years as he determined not only to excel with his thesis but also to learn to speak and write in English with excellence.

While Mau continued his graduate studies in Calgary, I was studying at the University of Alberta three hours away. I secretly wished I was backpacking across Europe like other people I'd met. Wouldn't that be incredible! But I didn't think I had the guts to do it. That was something only brave, adventurous people did, not people like me. Yet as I entered my third year of university, I realized that not only could I do it but I was actually going to make it happen. Some friends and I spent two months in the summer of 2003 traveling through seven European countries.

A month after arriving home, I woke up one day sensing that God wanted me to go back to China, this time for a longer stay. It's hard to explain—I suddenly *wanted* to go back even though I'd previously felt no desire to return. I asked God for direction, and He provided. By the time I completed my final year of school, I had already been hired to teach English at a university in southern China. This time, however, I was completely on my own. The personal stretching that I'd begun years before wasn't over yet.

+ + +

Around eleven o'clock at night, we receive word from the hospital that Nathaniel has been safely transferred to the children's hospital. We are ecstatic! The Lord has heard our prayers yet again—another small but important victory.

Emma and Thomas are both asleep, so we set out at once to visit Nathaniel. How interesting that I never would have left Thomas with anyone when he was a newborn, not even with my trustworthy parents, but I'm still being stretched in new ways.

"Don't worry, Christin," my mom assures me with an amused smile. "The kids will be just fine."

We hug by the front door, my parents in their pajamas, Mau and I in our winter jackets. Mau helps me ease my sore body into our car. At this time of night, a drive that would normally take forty-five minutes takes only twenty as we navigate the mostly deserted streets.

The hospital, normally bustling with doctors, patients, staff, and visitors, is eerily quiet as we take the main elevators up to the NICU. The young woman at the reception desk shows us where to sign in and explains the rules for entering through the doors that lead into the ward. We learn the guidelines for germ prevention and the limitations on visitors.

I authorize permission for five or six trusted friends, my parents, and two pastors to enter without Mau or me present. We wash our hands and wait as the woman at the desk opens the doors into the ward. The charge nurse points the way to Nathaniel's room down the hall.

There are four windowless rooms in this small wing, each with floor-to-ceiling drapes to provide privacy and keep out light. The sickest babies come here because it offers the quiet and darkness they require. On the glass door to Nathaniel's room is a card with his name on it, decorated like a scrapbook page with colorful animal stickers.

The room itself is somber and shadowed. We tiptoe up to Nathaniel's bed and look down at him as his nurse joins us. She welcomes us with a hushed tone and explains that Nathaniel managed the transfer well. Though his condition is currently stable, we get the impression that any noise, any light, or even a gentle touch could cause this fragile balance to topple like a house of cards. I gaze down at my little boy, grateful that I can now see his little face and body. Apart from the many tubes and sensors, he looks like a typical newborn—soft hair encircling his head, smooth skin with a pinkish tone, delicate fingers, and eyes squeezed shut.

Mau and I learn that Nathaniel is heavily sedated to prevent him from moving, a necessary provision that will keep him calm both now and after the surgery. The sedation will also allow him to heal without feeling pain or discomfort. After spending time praying for Nathaniel, we decide to head home for some sleep.

We're back again the next morning, this time with Emma and a diaper bag in my arms. A nurse finds a bassinet on wheels for Emma where she can have her naps when I'm with Nathaniel. While I sit nursing Emma, I begin to take in my surroundings. Nathaniel's ventilator hums softly, and indistinct voices drift in from outside the room. Every so often I hear the rustle of a page turning in Mau's Bible. I can't help but marvel at this newer NICU design, wherein families can stay with their children in relative comfort and privacy.

As I gently set Emma, belly full, in her bassinet, the nurse asks, "Would you like to touch Nathaniel?"

"Can I? It won't hurt him?" I reply, wide-eyed.

"He'll be all right. You can just place your hand on his leg. It's good for him to hear your voice and feel your touch."

"Okay . . . if you're sure."

I wash my hands again, determined not to let him catch any germs from me, and touch my son for the very first time. His leg is warm and soft. I'm filled with a tremulous joy, but as I turn my gaze from Nathaniel to the monitor, I can see that his heart rate is rising rapidly. I pull away my hand as fear grips my heart.

"That's okay; we gave it a try," says the nurse with compassion. "We can try again tomorrow if you like."

I nod in dubious agreement.

A short while later, a neonatologist comes by to give us an update. Mau and I move away from Nathaniel's bedside to listen. In a voice barely above a whisper, she says, "Nathaniel's adapting well after making the transfer from the hospital, which we knew would be quite stressful for him. But he made it, and he's doing better than expected." There's that phrase again—*better than expected.*

I wash my hands again, determined not to let him catch any germs from me, and touch my son for the very first time.

"When do you anticipate his surgery will be?" Mau asks. In our minds at least, the sooner the better.

"We'll need to see improvements in some areas before we can do the surgery," the doctor says. "We'd like to see Nathaniel's pulmonary and heart pressures improve and see him requiring less oxygen from the ventilator. We'd like to go into the surgery not depending as much on the medications, such as the one he is taking that helps with the contractions of his heart. The stronger he is beforehand, the less risky the surgery will be."

"So it won't be right away?" we ask.

"That's right. We're planning the surgery for next Tuesday or Wednesday."

Armed with this information, Mau sends out his next update to friends and family. He asks everyone to pray that Nathaniel can get stronger and stabilize enough to have the surgery. Our son has reached a tenuous balance, but will it last? Only time will tell. *Thank You, God, that You are our refuge and strength, a very present help in trouble* (Psalm 46:1).

CHAPTER 10

FEAR REARS ITS UGLY HEAD

"Blessed is the man who trusts in the LORD,
whose trust is the LORD.
He is like a tree planted by water,
that sends out its roots by the stream,
and does not fear when heat comes,
for its leaves remain green,
and is not anxious in the year of drought,
for it does not cease to bear fruit."

JEREMIAH 17:7-8

The early days in the children's hospital carry us along like a raft in turbulent waters. Mau and I settle into a new routine. Each morning we gather everything we'll need for a day at the hospital and then get everyone fed and dressed for the day. Mau has two weeks off from work, so I'm not alone in getting to and from the hospital with Emma and taking care of Thomas.

We're no longer staying at my parents' house, but they still come over every day, weekends included, to be with Thomas until his bedtime. They drive him to his preschool class, take him on outings, and help with meals, dishes, laundry, and much more. When Mau returns to work, which involves some weekends away, my parents are there for me. Another added blessing is the meal train organized by friends from church.

Every morning we maneuver our large double stroller into Nathaniel's NICU room and park it wherever we can find space. Though Thomas doesn't join us at the hospital often, he usually can't wait to visit because it means he can watch kids' shows on the big-screen TV in the children's play area—a treat he doesn't get at home. There is also a kitchenette with a fridge and a small table for eating. Mau or I place our lunch in the fridge while the other unbuckles Emma.

My strength is in Him, not in myself. Alone I'm weak, but in Him I'm strong.

I spend countless hours here feeding Emma, changing her diapers, and calming her down when she cries. While Mau devotes much of his time to praying and reading his Bible in Nathaniel's room, my time is mostly divided between the babies. I sit near and pray for Nathaniel whenever I can, but I also feel the guilt of never quite meeting *both* of their needs as well as I'd like. My favorite verse from Joshua replays often in my mind:

> "Have I not commanded you? Be strong and courageous. Do not be frightened, and do not be dismayed, for the Lord your God is with you wherever you go."
>
> JOSHUA 1:9

The verse is a constant reminder that God is with me, telling me not to fear. My strength is in Him, not in myself. Alone I'm weak, but in Him I'm strong. I hold tight to this powerful truth.

+ + +

A couple of days after Nathaniel's arrival, Mau and I are in the lounge with a friend who has come to visit when another woman enters. She overhears our conversation and makes a remark. As I turn to reply, I take in her appearance. She looks to be in her thirties with long hair swept up in a messy bun, strands jumping out in all directions, sweatpants, a hoodie, and no makeup—in other words, *NICU mom* is written all over her (just as anyone else would say of me). We introduce ourselves, and I learn that her name is Melissa.

"Do you have a little one here in the NICU?" Mau asks.

"Yes, his name is Greyson. He was born on March 8."

I do the math. That would make him about two weeks older than the twins.

"He came six weeks early and weighed just over two pounds," she says. She details some of the multiple health struggles he's come up against in addition to being a preemie.

"I'm so sorry," I say. "Poor little guy."

"And how are you handling everything?" Mau inquires.

Melissa says that Greyson is her only child, which means she's free to spend all her time at the hospital and can take a very active role in helping care for him. Most nights she sleeps on the couch in his room. Her husband works, but he visits when he can, although not nearly as much as she'd like.

"I'm not going to lie," she says. "It's been hard."

Mau, ever the pastor at heart, says, "Is there anything we can do for you? Please don't hesitate to ask us. We're part of a very supportive church, and I'm sure they'd love to help if you ever have any need." Melissa nods with a half smile, perhaps a bit skeptical.

"Can we pray for you?" Mau asks.

Though she's not a believer, she agrees, so we bow our heads as Mau prays. This is the first of many interactions with Melissa as our two sons fight to survive across the hall from each other.

+ + +

Nathaniel has two nurses assigned to him at all times. They work twelve-hour shifts that begin at either seven in the morning or seven at night. We get to know a couple of the nurses we see almost every day. Together, Amber and Evelyn seem to work without ceasing, attending to Nathaniel every time an alarm sounds from his monitor. I, however, feel like I'm still in a fog, unsure of what the lines and numbers on the monitors mean or why an alarm is sounding. All I know is that my little boy needs quiet, prayer, and his mother.

One day Amber hands me a small, soft cloth like the one that had been covering Nathaniel's head in the NICU.

"Here, put this in your shirt," she says. "Babies can recognize their mother's scent even before they're born. Nathaniel already knows yours, and it's the one he loves most. The cloth will pick up your scent, and when we put it on Nathaniel's head, it'll comfort him, and he'll feel nearer to you."

I keep it next to my skin for a while before we place it on his head. I take a second cloth home with me so that I can give him one fresh with my scent the next day.

"There's something else you can do for Nathaniel," Amber says. "Even though you can't breastfeed him, we can put a very small amount of breast milk in his cheek so that he still receives your antibodies. I've brought in a pump for you to use."

After pumping I watch as Amber uses a small syringe to put a tiny amount of breast milk into Nathaniel's mouth. I'm happy to have something to offer, small as it may be.

Every morning the medical team does their rounds. They confer about each tiny patient before moving on to the next, making their slow progression down the hallway. While Mau is off work, we're able to join in each day as they discuss Nathaniel. They listen to our questions and concerns without brushing us off and seem keen on keeping us in the loop. They don't sugarcoat Nathaniel's health status, but they always add a dollop of hope. Their hopeful perspectives stand in stark contrast to the hopeless prognosis offered to us by previous doctors.

"We all love Nathaniel," Amber says. "I don't know what it is, but he's just got such a special place in our hearts."

"He really does," agrees Evelyn.

These words are a balm to my soul, especially because other nurses will also say much the same thing.

That same day Evelyn introduces me to Beads of Courage, showing me a plastic bag with what looks like the makings of a beaded necklace inside. On a string I see several different colored beads plus a few that haven't been strung yet.

"Each different bead color represents a different treatment that Nathaniel has received," Evelyn explains, "so that by the time he's ready to leave he'll have a great reminder of what a fighter he is. We try to add to his strand each shift, but you're welcome to help us out."

It's a beautiful reminder, and I notice the string of beads growing in length as the days pass—a visual representation of my little boy's strength and God's hand in sustaining him.

On Saturday, five days after the twins' birth, my older sister, Jaci, and younger brother, Danny, both single with no kids of their own, arrive from Edmonton to meet their new niece and nephew. Mau and I take Jaci and Danny in to see Nathaniel, his room dark and quiet but for the hum of the equipment. My siblings are grateful to meet their newest nephew, and they smile as we quietly take a few pictures. Amber offers to let Danny lay his hand on Nathaniel's back, but moments later his heartbeat begins to accelerate at an alarming rate, the same way it did when I tried touching his leg.

A doctor informs us that Nathaniel had a good night and that the team will have a meeting on Monday to discuss his surgery, which is now scheduled for Wednesday, March 29. She also shares some good news—Nathaniel is now medicated only to keep him calm and comfortable, but he no longer requires medication to help with his pulmonary or cardiac pressures. This is a sign that he's more stable. Praise the Lord! The amounts of oxygen and nitric oxide (NO) he's receiving are still a bit high and should come down, but he no longer needs the maximum dosage.

On Monday morning we arrive at the NICU looking forward to participating in the regular meeting that afternoon. We're caught off guard, though, by a discussion that occurs before lunch. Mau and I have been in Nathaniel's room for a couple of hours when a nurse asks if we are available to meet with a certain doctor. We follow the nurse's directions to a drab, windowless room. The doctor enters, introduces himself, and dives into his prepared speech.

"Thank you for meeting with me. As you know, Nathaniel's operation is scheduled for Wednesday, and as I'm sure you're aware, his condition is quite delicate and uncertain. There are a number of risks involved with this surgery, and I'd like to bring one in particular to your attention."

He explains that there's a chance Nathaniel might experience either respiratory or pulmonary distress. The surgery team will exhaust every effort to stabilize him, he says, but if those efforts aren't sufficient, the team has one other option to use as a last resort. It's something called extracorporeal membrane oxygenation, otherwise known as ECMO.

"The patient is hooked up to a machine that allows their blood to bypass the lungs, which gives the lungs a chance to rest and heal. The machine removes the carbon dioxide from the blood and then oxygenates it, warms it, and returns it to the body."

Mau and I nod, listening intently. It's the first either of us has heard of this technology.

"Now, although ECMO is an option, I'd like to strongly dissuade you from choosing it. This therapy comes with serious risks that can lead to some very undesirable consequences. Of all babies who are put on ECMO, 50 percent do not survive. Of those who do survive, half of them will experience brain damage. That means that there's only a 25 percent chance that your son would make a full recovery."

Then he says words that rile Mau—words he'll never forget: "There are some things worse than death."

I'm someone who, in general, accepts what she's told, especially if it comes from someone in a position of authority. So in my mind, if the doctor says we shouldn't choose ECMO, then I'll likely respect his medical opinion. In this situation, I'm just beginning to think through the doctor's words.

I'm about to reply, "Well, in that case, we won't use ECMO," when Mau suddenly speaks up.

"We're people of life," he says, "so we'll always fight for life. If you're giving us a choice, then we'll choose ECMO if it comes to that."

I hear his words, but I'm dumbfounded. To be honest, I'm feeling rather confused and embarrassed. My brain struggles to process Mau's words. I turn to him and mumble, "Really? Why? You heard the odds. Shouldn't we do what the doctor says?"

"Why don't I give you some time to discuss this," the doctor suggests with no trace of emotion. "You can let the surgeon know what you decide when you speak with her later. If you'll excuse me."

This is the one and only time we'll see him—leaving us alone to make our biggest, most emotional decision since Nathaniel's birth.

As I consider the possibility of Nathaniel experiencing brain damage, my thoughts turn to a memorable analogy by author Emily Perl Kingsley, who gave birth to a child with Down syndrome. To illustrate this experience, Kingsley tells you to imagine that you've been planning a once-in-a-lifetime trip to Italy. You're all packed, your hotels are booked, and you're ready to go, but instead of landing in Italy, you find yourself in Holland. How disappointing! How did you end up there? It feels like a disaster. You now have to learn a new language, meet people you hadn't planned on meeting, and find new places to stay. Before long, though, you

"We're people of life," Mau says, "so we'll always fight for life."

realize that Holland is actually also a wonderful place with many interesting things to see and do. Italy isn't better; it's just different. You're left with an option: You can mourn the fact you never got to go to Italy, or you can choose to appreciate and make the most of your new destination.[1]

I agreed completely—of course a child with a disability is a gift of great worth and should be fully embraced. But in all my mental preparation for Nathaniel's arrival, I never factored in the possibility of a child with severe special needs. In my mind we would either go to Italy or not at all, but a trip to Holland was never on my radar. Had this been our initial prenatal diagnosis, I probably would have been devastated at first, but I like to think that I would have made the same choice to fight for my child's life no matter what. I would have turned to the Lord and His Word and come to the realization that God was still in control. I would trust that God would give us strength to welcome a baby with special needs, and we would love him with abandon.

But right now, today, the fear that Nathaniel could succumb to brain damage hits me hard, like an unexpected blow from behind. I can't catch my breath. Unlike any other moment in this journey, fear holds me in its viselike grip.

This must be why I learned that analogy! God was preparing me for this! Nathaniel's going to have brain damage! We're not going to make it to Italy. I wasn't prepared for this! Please, God, no!

I break down weeping, overcome by fear. Time passes. Mau tries to comfort me and understand my emotional turmoil. He shares his rationale for choosing ECMO, but my brain is muddled—nothing makes sense.

Finally my sobs abate. I'm spent, exhausted by raw emotion. As I wipe my tears the brain fog begins to lift. Mau explains once again why fighting for Nathaniel's life should include using ECMO if necessary. I begin to see that the course of action that offers the best chance of saving his life is the course of action we should take, just as we would have chosen life if we discovered early on that our child had a cognitive disorder. We won't let fear of the unknown make this decision for us, and I'm thankful that Mau's sight is clear enough for both of us. It strikes me later that Nathaniel's odds of survival from the beginning have always been about 25 percent, so why should the risks associated with ECMO feel any different? We'll leave this outcome in God's hands too.

I've often wondered why many expectant parents are prone to choose abortion at the first sign of trouble or why people believe "there are some things worse than death." Why is the death of a child, preborn or otherwise, preferable to letting that child live? I think it comes down to a non-Christian view of suffering. In other words, when the material world is all there is, the meaning of life becomes choosing whatever makes you happy.

Without God or a biblical understanding of suffering, most people have no idea how to cope when they're confronted with something as traumatic as a devastating prenatal diagnosis or even just the possibility of a child with a congenital defect. Society has offered them what seems like an easy out—a way to dispose of something that could lead to suffering and negatively affect their life trajectory. Their solution is abortion. Or in our case, withholding ECMO—a possibly lifesaving treatment—because a child with brain damage would hinder the parents' happiness and cause them to suffer, which of course must be avoided. If by eliminating the problem—even if that problem is a living human being—you can bypass suffering, then society says to by all means do it.

Plenty of people argue that it is compassionate and merciful to end the lives of those who suffer. Yet genuine compassion involves *suffering together*. That's why pro-lifers point out that compassion that refuses to suffer with another isn't compassion at all. Instead, in the name of mercy, it often advocates to end the life of the one who suffers. But death is not better than life, and abandoning the sufferer is not better than caring for them. It's true that we must do what we can to reduce suffering, but not by eliminating the one who suffers.

I reject the societal ideal that one's value is connected to what one can achieve or contribute to society. Our culture urges us to be the best—the smartest, strongest, most successful—and we want the same for our children. So heaven forbid that we should have a child who is weak or different, who isn't the smartest, strongest, or most successful! Yet I'm convinced that our value does not depend on what we can achieve. We are valuable for the simple reason that we are made in the image and likeness of God. His immeasurable love toward us doesn't change depending on our mental or physical attributes. We are valued and loved simply because we are His.

I'm convinced that our value does not depend on what we can achieve.

It's clear that the doctor we met with, like so many of his peers in the medical community, had embraced the ideologies of our times—and that I, in my vulnerable state, would have followed his lead. My heart goes out to the parents who find themselves in a similar head-reeling and hope-crushing situation.

Prior to the last several months, I had never experienced any significant hardships in life. I'd enjoyed a consistently happy life filled with loving relationships. I'd never been seriously ill, rejected, alone, abused, or in want. And despite my introverted nature, I had always approached the world with confidence, perhaps a bit naïve and overly optimistic in outlook. When I read verses like John 16:33 ("In the world you will have tribulation. But take heart; I have overcome the world."), I appreciated Jesus' words but figured I was somehow exempt from being one of those who have trouble. I knew trouble existed in the world, of course, but thought that I'd been spared, perhaps because I was extra blessed. As embarrassing as it is to admit now, I'd adopted the mentality that suffering wouldn't be a part of my life.

Boy, did I have some lessons to learn! Now in my forties, I look back on the past decade—one filled with untold hardships that hit me in rapid succession beginning with my pregnancy with the twins. Today I thank God that he allowed me to experience suffering. I was compelled to hold fast to the Lord like a small tree clinging to a cliffside in the middle of a storm. My untried faith was tested. I was forced to decide if I would continue to trust God even when life wasn't easy. Would I put my beliefs into practice?

God has a purpose for our suffering, and he has a purpose for each and every life. God wants to develop strength, wisdom, hope, and character in each of us as we care for others with true compassion.

+ + +

After washing my face and regaining my composure, I meet Nathaniel's surgeon, Dr. Smith, for the first time. She carries herself with quiet confidence, and I'm struck by her genuine warmth. It brings me assurance to know that she genuinely cares for Nathaniel's well-being. It's clear that she loves her job.

Dr. Smith and a host of other doctors—surgeons, cardiologists, neonatologists, and other specialists—gather around us to review the surgery plan. Later that evening, Mau sends out an update to anxious family members and friends. He quotes Scripture and describes the long journey ahead. Nathaniel is doing better than expected, he says, but we are not naïve. The surgery is risky, and our son is far from being out of harm's way. He then describes the procedure and lists several specific prayer requests for both during and after the surgery.

Mau concludes with gratitude: "I would like to thank all of you who have been praying for us and with us. Please continue to pray for life and for God's fame through it all! If you can, please join us as we fast, expressing our total dependence on God alone as the only source."

\+ + +

The day of the operation, Nathaniel's room is abuzz with activity as the team prepares to take him to the operating room. The next thing we know, we're part of the procession squeezing onto the elevator. I'm brimming with nervous jitters—this is the day Nathaniel will finally receive the surgery that's essential to his survival. Our extended family, friends, and church are praying. Nathaniel is as ready as he'll ever be for this day. Hope fills our hearts, but it doesn't quell the butterflies in our stomachs.

Hope fills our hearts, but it doesn't quell the butterflies in our stomachs.

Nathaniel is wheeled into the OR while we wait in the family lounge. The minutes pass like the slow drips of a melting icicle. Those drips then turn into hours. Mau reads his Bible and prays while I care for Emma, whispering simple prayers to distract from my worry. *When will we hear some news? How is Nathaniel withstanding the surgery?*

Around two o'clock someone tells us that Nathaniel has been brought back to his room. We quickly gather our things and head for the NICU. At least seven OR nurses wearing medical gear encircle Nathaniel's bed and obscure our view. When he is settled, the NICU nurses check lines, administer medication, and take note of the monitor's two-tone melody. Nathaniel lies unclothed with lines extending from his nose, left hand, right hand, and foot. I'm incredibly relieved to see him back in his room, alive and stable after what I can only imagine was a monumental feat.

Dr. Smith stops by soon after.

"Nathaniel did very well—better than expected."

There are those words again.

"Thank you so much," I say, unsure she could ever know how much I appreciate her years of study, training, and expertise.

Mau looks intently at the doctor and says, "I want you to know that more than three hundred people were praying for you and for Nathaniel."

Dr. Smith's eyes tear up in an instant and she smiles. "Thank you," she says. "That means a lot."

Mau sends out another update sharing the good news.

The Lord has answered yet another prayer this day. So many prayers, in fact, that I'm beginning to lose count. We return home with jubilant hearts, confident that Nathaniel has begun a steady road to recovery. We can't yet see the storms looming on the horizon.

CHAPTER 11

DARK CLOUDS

God is our refuge and strength,
a very present help in trouble.
Therefore we will not fear though the earth give way,
though the mountains be moved into the heart of the sea.

PSALM 46:1–2

The first couple of days post-op pass with positive updates from the doctors. Nathaniel is able to eliminate fluids, a sign that his kidneys are functioning, and the doctors plan to start reducing some medications and the nitric oxide. So far so good. But on the morning of Saturday, April 1, we arrive to learn from Amber that Nathaniel had a difficult night and needed a large dose of medication to increase the blood flow to his brain and other organs to prevent organ damage.

The doctor overseeing Nathaniel's care finds us in his room.

"If you'll look here, you can see that Nathaniel's abdomen is discolored," she says. "We think his liver might have an infection, so we're going to start him on some broad-spectrum antibiotics. He was manipulated a lot last night, which caused him some agitation, so we're going to handle him as little as possible today and try to keep him nice and calm."

Nathaniel isn't producing much urine, nor is he tolerating being touched or handled by the nurses. Each movement triggers the monitor alarms. On Sunday Nathaniel is slightly more stable, but it's a fragile stability. His stomach has been filling with air, which makes it difficult for him to breathe. As a result, he now has two lines of intubation—one through his mouth that leads to his lungs so he can breathe and the other going from his nose to his stomach to remove excess air. On an encouraging note, an X-ray reveals that Nathaniel's right lung has already expanded a little.

Later in the day Mau composes another group message: "We don't know what the Lord is doing, but let's keep crying out to the Lord of glory."

We can't fathom the extent to which Nathaniel's struggles are about to worsen. The next two weeks find us crying out repeatedly to the Lord as we wait for even the faintest glimmer of hope while his condition takes a terrifying turn.

+ + +

"A typhoon's coming. Classes are canceled tomorrow. Go home, stay indoors, and stay safe."

I'd been teaching English at a university in southern China for a number of months and was loving every minute of it. At age twenty-two, I was full of energy, developing my teaching skills, and befriending both American and Chinese colleagues. One day while playing basketball, I happened to meet the members of a student band. As a mediocre piano player and decent singer, I found myself joining their practices. I tried Chinese calligraphy, sword dancing, tennis, and more. I was living a life of adventure.

I looked up at the sky. Blue. Sunny. *A typhoon's coming? Really? This is going to be interesting.*

As an Albertan prairie girl, I was experienced at living through (and driving through) blizzards in the winter and thunderstorms in the summer, but a typhoon? I felt a bit of excitement in my chest. I walked from the teaching building toward my home in one of the faculty apartment buildings. There I hurried up several flights of stairs—elevators were scarce in this town—to my two-bedroom apartment, courtesy of Shantou University.

I looked out the window. No change. But eventually the wind started to blow. Clouds rolled in from the coast and raindrops began to fall. Darkness descended, and within minutes, the fury of the tempest was unleashed.

I watched in awe as rain blew sideways against the panes of glass with such ferocity that it was like someone had pointed massive hoses at each window. I felt tremors through the solid concrete floor as the wind lashed at the building like a raging monster. I watched in fear as water started pouring in through the poorly sealed windows. My fifth-floor apartment was at risk of flooding! I quickly got to work with my mop, bucket, and every towel I owned. *Soak up the water, wring out the water, repeat.* I worked for hours until, exhausted, I fell asleep to the sound of screaming wind and pounding rain, hoping and praying I wouldn't wake up in a wading pool.

Hours later I awoke to sunlight streaming in through a crack in the curtains. My floor was dry. Debris covered the streets, and the reservoir was so full that students were catching fish with their bare hands. Life returned to normal for all but the street sweepers, who had their work cut out for them in the days that followed. I had survived my first typhoon.

+ + +

The storm I'm in now, on the twins' second-week birthday, is nothing like that typhoon of 2005. There's nothing exciting about it. There's no sunlight through the curtains. There's no running home gleefully with a fish in your hands. Mau's latest message starkly contrasts his usual verbose updates:

> Nathaniel is not well—very unstable. Please ask people to pray. He continues to have problems breathing, his heart rate keeps falling, and he's in a lot of pain.

We keep vigil by Nathaniel's bed with furrowed brows, apprehensively monitoring the monitors. We step aside each time an alarm sounds, calling the nurses in again and again to suction fluid out of our baby boy's lungs so he can breathe. We stand by powerless, unable to help our son in any way save to watch and pray. Amber and Evelyn are again working together today, and the worry on their faces betrays the seriousness of Nathaniel's critical state. We later learn that these two angels are putting in an extra hour at the end of every shift to catch up on the paperwork they're unable to complete during their normal shift. That's because they're working nonstop to keep our son alive.

"Nathaniel is not well."

The days that follow meld into one long, wearisome nightmare. Nathaniel is in the fight of his young life. An infection is wreaking havoc on his body, yet the doctors have no idea what it is or where it's coming from. He is no longer able to eliminate fluids, and his body is puffed up like a balloon. His skin has lost its healthy pink glow, replaced by an unnatural gray pallor. Swollen eyes and lips give his face a bloated, fishlike quality. A somber hush pervades his room; the doctors and nurses are afraid to put into words what they fear.

By God's grace I remain unaware of how dire the situation is. My mom and dad, who come to pray, somehow know how bad things look. Nathaniel needs a miracle. Like a car teetering on the edge of a cliff, Nathaniel's life hangs in the balance. If I were in a less bewildered state of mind, seeing Nathaniel like this would surely reduce me to tears. Instead I shuffle like a phantom from one moment to the next.

Somehow we make our way to the hospital each day. Somehow I take care of Emma's needs despite how overwhelmed I feel, nursing her and putting her down for naps in Nathaniel's hospital room. I whisk her away the moment she makes the tiniest peep because Nathaniel, in this fragile state, can't handle any loud noises. Somehow I continue to take care of my darling girl, even though I want nothing more than to remain at Nathaniel's bedside nonstop. Somehow we make it home each evening. For the first time since childhood I fall asleep moments after my head hits the pillow.

Like a car teetering on the edge of a cliff, Nathaniel's life hangs in the balance.

Despite the exhausting emotional weight of this ordeal, we can sense the prayers of God's people. We should be overcome by worry, stress, and grief, and yet Mau and I both feel like we're being carried—the burden is there, but we are being spared the crushing effects of its weight. Though I'm at the end of my human rope, I'm nonetheless buoyed, my head lifted above the waters of this raging river. I remember how Jesus calmed a raging storm that His disciples were sure would be the end of them. In their humanity they were terrified, but God was with them, so they had no reason to fear. Neither do I.

Even with this comfort from the Lord, I barely manage to provide basic care for Emma and Thomas, nothing more. Mau continues to spend time in God's Word and prayer, each day sending out detailed updates on Nathaniel's condition via social media. We hear reports that one church after another has been praying—first from our city, then from other provinces and as far away as Brazil. Mau's Facebook posts are being shared far and wide, and family, friends, and strangers are pleading with the Lord to reach down and save our boy. We have not seen the results of these prayers yet, but—despite grim reports from the doctors—we have not lost hope.

+ + +

One afternoon I run into Melissa in the family lounge.

"I'm sorry Nathaniel's been struggling these past several days," she says. "For once Greyson isn't the sickest baby in the NICU."

I'm confused and a little surprised. "How did you know?" I didn't think Mau or I had seen her for a while.

"You know—the monitors in their rooms show the vitals of all four patients in our hallway. I can see each time that Nathaniel desats." (*Desats*, or *desaturates*, I learn, means that the oxygen levels in his blood dip dangerously low, triggering an alarm.)

I've been too preoccupied to try deciphering the meaning of

each line on the monitor other than heart rate and blood pressure. Melissa seems surprised that I don't know, but eventually I'll learn that desaturation below 90 percent is quite worrisome, and less than 80 percent is cause for extreme intervention.

On Wednesday Mau notifies our prayer partners:

> Nathaniel has been heavily sedated so the doctors can have full access to his body without any fluctuation in his breathing or pain. His body has retained a lot of fluid from the surgery, which has also been accentuated because of the infection. The doctors still don't know what type of infection he has or where the source is. . . . His kidneys are working fine, but the fluid isn't getting there to be filtered and eliminated, and the more fluid, the better the environment in his body for the infection to keep growing.
>
> In short, we need to pray that the infection will disappear. The infection is causing everything.

The following day, Thursday, April 6, a new nurse informs us that Nathaniel is faring a bit better. His toleration for being handled by the doctors and nurses has improved, and it seems that the antibiotics are beginning to fight off the infection. He's still highly sedated, but the fact that he isn't getting worse is like the first blossom of spring after a long, cold winter.

Nathaniel's blood vessels are now starting to absorb the extra liquid in his body, and he's begun producing some urine again. Praise God! But we're also alerted to a couple of new concerns: Nathaniel is only receiving the minimum nutrition necessary to survive, not what he requires for growth in general and his lungs in particular. And because of his swollen body, the doctors are having difficulty finding a vein to put a second line in to provide this nutrition. There's also some concern over his liver, which may have been the source of the infection because it was manipulated during the surgery. An ultrasound is inconclusive, but Nathaniel's skin begins to take on a yellowish hue that seems to point to liver damage.

We send out yet more calls for specific prayer.

By Saturday we're relieved to see that Nathaniel has attained a level of stability that we haven't seen since just after his surgery. The nurses are no longer rushing in and out of his room, responding to one alarm after another for twelve hours straight. For the first time since our son's birth, the lights in the room are on and his face is no longer covered by the small cloth with my scent. Yet our precious boy still looks so vulnerable—yellowish skin, puffy eyes closed tight, swollen lips and abdomen, and a partially shaved head that has developed an elongated shape from his being laid on one side and then the other but never flat on his back.

"How would you feel about trying some kangaroo care today?" Evelyn asks me as we gaze down at Nathaniel in his Isolette, Emma napping peacefully nearby.

"Sure, if you think he can handle it," I reply, though my mind returns to those early days when barely touching our son caused his heart rate to skyrocket.

When a baby is born, especially a baby in the NICU, both the mother and father are encouraged to hold their baby close for skin-to-skin contact. Kangaroo care can provide many benefits for the baby, such as stabilized breathing and heart rate, increased weight gain, improved oxygen saturation, improved quality and duration of sleep, and increased parent-infant bonding.

The thought of finally being close to Nathaniel and knowing how it might benefit him ignites my enthusiasm. Evelyn gets me a blue hospital gown and helps draw the curtain around the couch. She lowers the side of Nathaniel's Isolette and helps me position myself, my chest resting gently against his side. I'm leaning over and looking down at my baby like a mother hen whose chick is nestled beneath her protective wings. This nearness, combined with Nathaniel's warmth and sweet baby scent, is a treasured gift. And this time, at last, he's able to tolerate the physical touch.

The position I'm standing in is awkward, and my body is still a little sore from giving birth, so our skin-to-skin bonding time doesn't last long. But Evelyn has another delightful surprise in store—she suggests we lay Emma beside Nathaniel in his bed for a little while as she sleeps. It will be the first time they've been near each other since sharing my womb. I let Evelyn do the honors, concerned about upsetting one wire or another. Next thing I know, there they are together—a rosy little girl dressed in a sleeper with pink hearts and a frail little boy dressed in nothing but a diaper over dull skin. My twins are reunited. I hope in my heart that this will be the first of many times they'll be together.

Later that day, Mau sends out a message filled with hope:

> "So the LORD was with Joshua" (Joshua 6:27).
>
> The Lord is with Nathaniel Joshua, too. And we know this because Nathaniel is here with us. Praise the Lord for His presence with us! The greatest Joshua, Yeshua, Emmanuel, Jesus the Christ, is with Nathaniel and with us.

The doctors hope in the next few days to remove the medication that is keeping him paralyzed so that he will be able to breathe on his own. Keeping him more sedated over the next few days should also help his CO_2 and O_2 levels. We pray that the Lord will protect his organs and brain after being on so much medicine.

The twins are now almost three weeks old, and it's been a week and a half since Nathaniel's surgery, but it feels like the hospital is the only existence we've ever known. The ride we're on, with its relentless twists and turns (and nosedives!), has been hurtling us forward without a chance to catch our breath. Could it be that perhaps the ride is beginning to slow down? Could the terrifying ordeal of infection and failing organs be behind us? Can we pause to take a breath? We continue to hope—hope for healing and hope to one day bring Nathaniel home.

It's been a week and a half since Nathaniel's surgery, but it feels like the hospital is the only existence we've ever known.

CHAPTER 12

"YOUR EYES ARE BEAUTIFUL, MY SON"

Behold, children are a heritage from the LORD,
the fruit of the womb a reward.
PSALM 127:3

The new week dawns with promise and hope. Spring is in the air as snow melts and the afternoon sun shines down on upraised faces. Green grass and tulips begin to appear, bringing with them the fresh scent of new growth.

Mau, Emma, and I enter Nathaniel's room, happy to see steady numbers on the monitor. Our son looks the same—yellow and swollen, silent and unmoving—but there has been a shift in his condition. The doctor on duty joins us to give us the daily update.

"I'm happy to tell you that Nathaniel has been making some improvement," she says. "You can see here"—she points to the monitor of the ventilator machine—"that we've been able to drop his oxygen requirements to 30 percent."

"What exactly does that mean?" I ask.

"It means his lungs are doing more of the work of breathing, which is very good. We'd like to see his oxygen requirements continue to decrease as his lungs do more and more of the work on their own. We've also been able to lower his nitric oxide levels."

She tells us that they've taken a chest X-ray that showed a lot of fluid on Nathaniel's right side, which is compressing his smaller lung there. It appears, however, that the lung is trying to expand, so once the fluid drains, his right lung will have room to grow.

"We've started decreasing the amount of muscle relaxant we've been administering so his limbs can start moving," the doctor adds. "This will allow his body to move excess fluid into his tissues so that it can be eliminated. We need to keep him on the pain medications for a considerable amount of time though. Our plan is to wean him off the relaxers first, then the sedation, then the painkillers."

"How long do you expect this whole process to take?" we wonder.

"It's still going to be several weeks."

It's a lot of news to take in. The healing process will take a long time, but praise God that it's underway. Nathaniel's current condition is much improved compared to where he was a week and a half ago. I assume the doctor is about to wrap up her report, but she hasn't quite finished.

"One concern we still have now is Nathaniel's liver function. He has jaundice, and his liver is still having trouble." She pauses as she looks over at Nathaniel. "Once a second line is in, we'll start giving Nathaniel the lipids he needs to grow and a medication that will help his liver function."

The next day a NICU nurse tells us that since they've been

lowering the amount of relaxant Nathaniel's receiving, she's noticed him trying to breathe on his own. From no breathing capability at birth to the beginnings of it now is a marvel to us.

On Thursday, April 13, the twins are twenty-four days old. The atmosphere in Nathaniel's room is celebratory as a once very ill infant is showing signs of life. The little boy who wasn't supposed to survive is getting a little better each day. To our great joy, we see Nathaniel move on his own for the first time. His delicate fingers furl and unfurl, his mouth opens and closes, and his arms and legs make small movements.

Amber enters his room with a big smile. "Isn't Nathaniel looking well?" she says. "I saw his eyes open this morning—they're so beautiful!—and he was looking around at everything."

"That's amazing!" Mau says. "Too bad we missed it. And yes, he *is* starting to look better. What a miracle!" I grin in agreement.

"Should we try to wake him up?" Amber asks.

"Definitely!" I reply.

Amber removes the little cloth that is resting on Nathaniel's head and begins to gently stroke his crown.

"Nathaniel, wake up," I croon as he tries to open his eyes. "Yeah, there you go! Can you open your eyes? I love you." I pause for several seconds. "Hey, little one," I say with a smile.

"He's trying," Amber says, and I smile again watching the movement of Nathaniel's eyes beneath his eyelids. He's working so hard to open them.

"Wake up, baby. There you go—almost. Almost . . ."

"Oh, so close!"

We decide to try again tomorrow but are encouraged by the improvements he's made.

Mau's update expresses gratitude for Nathaniel's progress and once again asks for prayer:

> Today Nathaniel was at 26 percent oxygen, which is quite good because we all breathe at 21 percent, so he's almost at a normal level. Also, we praise God that he is no longer on the medicine that paralyzed him and that they're now using this line to give him lipids—the nutrition we have been praying for so that he can grow!
>
> The doctors are still worried about his liver. The ultrasound appears to reveal a portion of it that may have become necrotic, which if confirmed will have to be removed.
>
> Please pray with us that Nathaniel will continue to stabilize, adjust to being off the medication, and develop and grow. Also please pray for healing in his liver—for a full recovery to surprise us and the doctors.

The journey we've been on thus far has been difficult and has tested our faith. My response could be to curse God and shake my fist at Him for allowing us to go through this ordeal. Or my response could be one of perseverance—continuing day after day despite the overwhelming fear, fatigue, and stress.

Mau and I have chosen to persevere, knowing that "weeping may tarry for the night, but joy comes with the morning" (Psalm 30:5). When I keep my eyes on Jesus, on His sacrifice and the strength He has given me through His Spirit, I can continue without giving up.

Would it have been easier to abort Nathaniel? In some ways, yes. We wouldn't have faced the scorn of the doctors or the stress we're enduring now. But in every other way, no. The so-called easy path doesn't seem so easy after hearing the accounts of many women who've faced the emotional and medical distress that often follows an abortion. Nor does it account for the truth that taking a life violates God's moral law. Indeed, many times it's the difficult path that leads to faith, hope, strength, triumph, and joy. The difficult path is the one that leads to character, to reassurance, and to no regrets. And though our difficult days are far from over, I'd choose this path every time.

The difficult path is the one that leads to character, to reassurance, and to no regrets. . . . I'd choose this path every time.

+ + +

Good Friday is here, and with it my siblings are visiting again from Edmonton. Thomas, who has a hard time sitting still and has developed a cold, stays in the family lounge to watch cartoons with my father while the rest of us are in Nathaniel's room. Someone has delivered a helium balloon that says "Happy Easter" and a little stuffed ducky. The relaxed, lighthearted atmosphere stands in stark contrast to the tension of Jaci and Danny's previous visit.

"Look, Mau! Look!" I exclaim in excitement as Mau and I gaze at Nathaniel. He's still yellow and puffy, but he's moving. "There you go, buddy," I murmur as Nathaniel blinks and looks around as if just awaking from a nap. *His eyes! I've just seen his eyes for the very first time!* "Your eyes are beautiful, my son!" I say as he yawns wide and rests his eyelids for several moments before opening them again.

The doctor says they've been able to reduce some of his

medications, oxygen, and nitric oxide to the lowest levels yet, and the respiratory therapist says his blood levels are so good that it almost looks like the report is a mistake. Nathaniel even has a box in his bed that makes background noise so he can get used to outside sounds.

The next day, while Nathaniel sleeps, I hold up a small vial of breast milk attached to a tube that enters his nose and extends down his throat into his stomach. This is the first attempt to feed him directly into his stomach.

As I leave Nathaniel's room with Emma in my arms, I pass Melissa in the hallway as she returns to her son's room.

"How's it going?" I ask. "How is Greyson doing?"

"He has his ups and downs," she sighs. "Today's been a bit frustrating, actually."

Melissa expresses concerns about Greyson's treatment, wondering if the doctors should be doing things differently. Trying to steer the conversation in a more positive direction, I inquire, "Have you been working on Greyson's Beads of Courage?"

"Yes, I string his beads pretty much every day," she says. "The string is already about ten feet long. Greyson is a little warrior; there's no doubt about that." She beams with the pride of a devoted mother.

The weight of Emma and the diaper bag is causing pain in my still-healing back, so I excuse myself, sure that our paths will cross again.

As Mau and I drive home, I bring up something that's been on my mind.

"Now that Nathaniel is more awake and we can't be with him at the hospital all the time, I'm a bit worried that he'll feel lonely. The nurses can't be there with him all the time," I say.

"I'm also concerned that I'm not bonding with him the same way that I have with Emma. She gets to be with us all the time—I nurse her, and she's always being held and cuddled, while poor Nathaniel is all by himself, and I can't hold him." I want to be there for both my babies, and I'm beginning to feel guilty that I've bonded with Emma but not Nathaniel.

"I hear what you're saying," Mau says. "We added the names of some friends and family to the visitation list, so maybe we should ask if they'd be able to visit him when we're not there."

"Good idea—and we could start a WhatsApp group to coordinate visits," I reply, feeling the weight lifting. I don't know how invaluable this group will become over the next couple of weeks.

On Easter Sunday, I wake up with a tickle in my throat. Thomas has been fighting something, so I've probably caught whatever he has. The NICU has made it very clear that we shouldn't visit if we're sick, and being the rule abider that I am, I stay home to avoid the risk of getting Nathaniel sick. Mau visits the hospital on his own after church, and he finds Nathaniel very alert.

"You're awake! You're so beautiful, son," Mau says. Just then the monitor starts beeping.

A nurse comes in response, but the monitor is clearly not a major concern. "Can you tell him to behave?" she asks Mau with a smile.

Now that Nathaniel's condition has begun to improve, he has been reclassified as a level 2 patient, down from level 3, which is reserved for the most critically ill. He only has one dedicated nurse instead of two, and we've been seeing a number of different nurses, not just Amber and Evelyn.

"How was your church service?" asks the nurse.

"It was great! There's nothing better than celebrating Jesus on Easter."

"Absolutely," she agrees.

The following day offers Mau and me an uplifting gift: We meet a woman and her four-year-old daughter, a child who was also born with CDH and was treated at this very same hospital. I'm immediately struck by how healthy this little girl appears. Long, wavy blonde hair hangs down her back, and shy blue eyes look up at us as we introduce ourselves. She heads off to the play area as we converse with her mom.

We learn that her daughter stayed in the hospital for twelve weeks yet eventually went home without any ventilation or feeding tubes. They are believers, and we're comforted by their story, but it is the little girl herself—tangible evidence that CDH kids do survive—that bolsters my faith to believe that one day we'll see Nathaniel living and thriving in the same way.

Due to the lingering tickle in my throat, after our conversation I remain in the family lounge with Emma while Mau visits Nathaniel in his room. The doctors seem very pleased with his progress. They've removed his stitches and are planning to extubate him next week. They've reduced his painkillers. His puffiness is being reduced because he's eliminating fluids well. He still has some fluid in the right side of his chest, but there are no plans to drain any fluid at this time due to the risk of infection. They've started to bottle-feed him milk, increasing the amount each time, and he is getting used to it. The great unknown is still Nathaniel's liver, so they're continuing to watch it to determine a course of action.

As Tuesday dawns, the feeling in my throat remains. *What am I going to do? I haven't seen Nathaniel for two days already. The last thing he needs is to catch a virus from me, but he also needs me. Mau is back at work now and can't spend the day at the hospital.*

This is the start of a heart-wrenching time for me. For the next two weeks I stay away from the hospital to help keep Nathaniel safe. Though the tickle never turns into anything more, and though I want nothing more than to be with my son, my desire to protect him is even stronger.

I call the NICU and speak to his nurse just to make sure that staying away is in fact the best course of action.

"That's tough," she agrees, "but I think it'd be best if you don't come in."

The days pass and begin to pile up. How can I even begin to express the anguish I feel each day that I don't get to see my son? I'm gripped by feelings of helplessness and sadness. Going about daily life with Thomas and Emma feels like torment when my Nathaniel is tethered to his hospital bed.

God, please, help me get better so I can go back to the hospital. Please be with Nathaniel—don't let him be lonely. Please comfort him for me when I can't be there for him. Thank You, Lord, for Your care and provision.

As I cast my cares about Nathaniel on Jesus, knowing that He is holding Nathaniel and will not let him go, the Lord fills me with assurance.

+ + +

We've all heard the old proverb "It takes a village to raise a child." Well, I'm glad to say that our family's village comes together to support Nathaniel now that Mau has returned to work and I'm forced to keep my distance. My parents and several friends from church take turns visiting the hospital, and they send me pictures and videos from their visits. These two weeks are full of small victories that I watch from afar as our little boy takes incremental steps toward recovery.

On April 19, just a day before Nathaniel turns one month old, the team extubates him. And Mau is there to witness it.

"One, two, three," a nurse counts as they slide the ventilation tube from his lungs, and then the nurse greets Nathaniel with a bright "Hello!"

"There we go," says another as our boy coughs and takes his first unaided breaths. She suctions his mouth and swiftly inserts some nasal prongs that will supply him with supplemental oxygen.

The poor little guy doesn't know what has hit him! He takes big breaths with his gaping mouth, a deep frown etched on his face. A few faint cries reach their ears.

"There's a voice box!" says a nurse. "There you go!"

With each breath the skin beneath his rib cage sucks in. Each inhale is a mighty effort. His legs, scrawny again after shedding excess fluid, pump up and down in alarm. His inaudible cries would be piercing screams in a healthy baby, but the nurses don't seem shaken in the least. They know this is a necessary part of the treatment plan.

"Sometimes it can take a bit for them to get their voices back because that tube was between their vocal cords for so long," a nurse tells Mau. "But the good news is that he doesn't have any high-pitched squeaking, so we know they're not too swollen."

Learning to breathe and swallow for himself is a major endeavor. The doctors and nurses make Nathaniel as comfortable as possible, but after a few hours they decide that he's having to work too hard and reintubate him. They explain that the effort Nathaniel is making to breathe would be like ours if we were trying to breathe at the top of Mount Everest.

Each inhale is a mighty effort. . . . His inaudible cries would be piercing screams in a healthy baby.

They try again on April 22. Mau is away on a business trip, so neither parent is by Nathaniel's side. This time, however, he remains extubated! A thoughtful nurse sends us a short video. ("Nathaniel, say hello to mama!") In place of the tubes that used to go down his throat, Nathaniel is chomping on a bright orange pacifier, and a little teddy bear plays music from the corner of the bed. The merry sounds can't erase the grimace on Nathaniel's face, but this little guy has a God given will to survive, to fight on, to take another breath. He's too young to feel defeated.

When Mau arrives home the next day and visits Nathaniel, he's met with a surprise.

"Would you like to hold him?" asks the nurse.

"Are you serious? That'd be amazing!"

Mau is overcome with joy; his face beams with a mixture of awe and gratitude as he cradles his dear boy. The nurse takes some pictures; then Mau makes a video in Portuguese to send to friends and family.

"Papai 'ta segurando Nathaniel pela primeira vez. Que alegria!" ("Daddy is holding Nathaniel for the first time. What joy!")

My parents are the next ones to hold him. My mom settles herself in the armchair and gathers her grandson into her arms for the first time, my dad standing nearby. Nathaniel moves his head around as though trying to figure out what's going on around him.

"Hi, Nathaniel, it's Grandma. I see you moving around so that you can hear everything in the hallway. You're getting so strong!" She and my dad smile down at him, savoring the moment.

Mau's latest update says:

> The doctors are slowly taking Nathaniel's medication away, and his oxygen level is now 21 percent, which is wonderful because that's what we breathe! He still has fluid enclosing his right lung, the smaller lung, which is impeding its growth, so please pray for this fluid to go. . . . Please pray for his liver, that the doctors will have the wisdom and clarity they need.

Each day Nathaniel makes progress, gaining more use of his lungs, feeling less pain, and becoming more alert. Despite my continued angst over being separated from him, our spirits are buoyed, grateful to the Lord for the healing work He's doing. We can't see it, of course, but our world is about to be turned upside down once more.

CHAPTER 13

BACK TO SQUARE ONE

Even though I walk through the valley of the shadow of death,
I will fear no evil,
for you are with me;
your rod and your staff,
they comfort me.

PSALM 23:4

On April 28 Mau is scheduled to lead workshops at a men's retreat in a small town in northern Alberta, a place so far north that it gets very few visitors. It's so small and remote that flying isn't an option; the only way to get there is a twelve-hour drive from our home. Having made this trek twice before, Mau invites two friends to join him to help pass the time. They depart early Friday morning on what should be an uneventful road trip.

I don't go to church this particular Sunday. Without Mau by my side, the entire affair is a stressful ordeal with a newborn and a preschooler. Around eleven in the morning I receive a call from one of Nathaniel's nurses.

"Christin, I'm afraid I have some bad news," she says. "Nathaniel became agitated during the night. We weren't sure at first what was wrong, but we took an X-ray and discovered that he reherniated. His intestines have moved back up into his chest, so he needs surgery as soon as possible to repair the patch. How soon can you get here? We need you to sign the papers giving permission for the surgery."

The room spins. Panic sets in. Mau is hundreds of kilometers away, and the kids and I are nowhere near ready. My mind races as I think about the process required for me to leave the house: children to dress, diapers to change, bottles to prepare.

"Okay," I reply, but inside I'm reeling. "I'll be there as soon as I can."

Never one to remain calm in a crisis, I try to call Mau. I get his voicemail. I leave a panicked message. I try again. Still no answer. I send a text begging him to call, explaining the situation. I figure he's already been on the road for a few hours and is probably in the middle of nowhere on his way back home. Besides, there's nothing he can do right now.

Never one to remain calm in a crisis, I try to call Mau. I get voicemail. I leave a panicked message. I try again. Still no answer. I send a text begging him to call.

So I call my mother. Thank goodness she answers. I explain the situation, words pouring out of my mouth in a frenzied spray, and she assures me that she and Dad will be right over. Dad will take Thomas for the day, and Mom will join me at the hospital. I begin to tear around, grabbing this, packing that. I scramble to change out of my sweatpants, throw my hair into a messy bun, and get Thomas and Emma ready.

I think about Nathaniel struggling to breathe, about to endure another major surgery. Tears begin to fall. It's hard to understand why this has happened; he was taking such wonderful strides!

Lord, please protect Nathaniel. Please help him get through this.

My phone rings. Praise the Lord, it's Mau!

"So what's going on?" he asks. "Nathaniel reherniated? Do they know how it happened? Are you at the hospital yet?" He shouts rapid-fire questions over the rumbling of the highway. The apprehension is evident in his voice.

"I don't know much of anything," I explain, "just that it happened last night sometime. I think the patch ruptured. I'm about to get Emma in the car, and Thomas will go with my dad. They should be here any minute. How far are you from Calgary?"

"We're still seven hours away," he sighs. "We're trying to go as fast as we can."

"Okay, I'll do my best to keep you in the loop. Drive safe, and I'll talk to you soon. I've got to keep going here."

"We'll be praying," he says.

Mau prays: *God, please let me arrive safely in Calgary; be with Christin as she's dealing with this situation. And please be with Emma and Thomas as well. Dear Lord, please protect and save Nathaniel's life; shelter him under Your wings.*

I greet my parents with a frazzled hello. I wave goodbye to Thomas as my mother and I hop in my car and take off in a rush.

From far away Mau sends out another update:

Nathaniel is not well; he'll have to have another operation. We're back to square one.

+ + +

The night Mau proposed to me I had no voice. It wasn't just because I was overwhelmed by the moment—I had been teaching kindergarten since the beginning of the school year, and let's just say that it wasn't going well. I dreaded going to the school each day, my stomach constantly in knots. In this anxious state I lost my voice, and for two months I was unable to teach at all. It was actually a relief.

Despite my lack of speech, Mau still came around, kind and supportive as always, and we started planning our wedding. Five months later we were married on a perfect summer day in a perfectly quaint church surrounded by perfectly supportive family and friends.

Soon after, however, the reality of marriage hit. It was like opening a gift basket only to realize it was half-filled with packaging. There was nothing particularly wrong with Mau, and there was nothing particularly wrong with me—save for the fact that we were (and still are) two perfectly imperfect, selfish people.

Sometimes life was good, but more often it was hard. Mau and I, though both well meaning, had very different ideas about how we should live our lives as a married couple. Like two pieces of sandpaper, we sometimes rubbed each other the wrong way. Other times we got stuck.

After giving up on teaching kindergarten, I got a job teaching employment skills to young immigrant mothers. There I thrived. Though I wasn't following my passion to travel the world, in a sense the world had come to me. Mau still designed homes and won awards back then, but the Lord was stirring his heart to move into full-time Christian ministry.

As time passed, our sandpaper began to smooth, and we got stuck less often. Marriage wasn't easy, but it wasn't as hard as in the beginning. I still had a lot to learn about life and marriage and hardship and the goodness of God. I didn't realize it at the time, but I needed refining. Perhaps God, in His kindness, had a plan to stretch me in ways that would make me rely on Him and Him alone.

In the beloved novel-turned-movie *The Princess Bride*, author William Goldman introduces fifteen-year-old Buttercup as merely ranking among the top twenty most beautiful women in the world. But after she learns about the death of her true love, Westley, and grieves in her room for many days, she reappears changed:

> In point of fact, she had never looked as well. She had entered her room as just an impossibly lovely girl. The woman who emerged was a trifle thinner, a great deal wiser, an ocean sadder. This one understood the nature of pain, and beneath the glory of her features, there was character, and a sure knowledge of suffering.
>
> She was eighteen. She was the most beautiful woman in a hundred years.[1]

Perhaps, if we would allow it, suffering could bring out the beauty in all of us.

+ + +

The journey to the hospital this morning is like one of those nightmares in which you want to run but can't. Try as you might, you can't move any faster than a snail. Mom and I finally make it to the hospital nearly two hours after receiving the nurse's call.

I dart over to the receptionist to find out what's happening.

"They're waiting for you in Nathaniel's room."

My mother and I scrub in. This is the first time in two weeks that I'm entering the NICU since my throat started bothering me. A nurse I haven't met before greets me in Nathaniel's doorway.

"Could I please have a mask?" I ask, full of concern. "I haven't been in to see Nathaniel for two weeks because of a tickle in my throat, but I have to see him, and I don't want to get him sick."

The nurse hesitates, but she finds me one even though I probably shouldn't be here. Multiple nurses and a respiratory therapist prepare Nathaniel for his transfer to the operating room. Someone hands me a clipboard with the permission form, which I sign immediately. A tall man dressed in blue scrubs enters and makes a beeline to me. He introduces himself as Nathaniel's surgeon. I wonder why I don't see Dr. Smith, his previous surgeon.

The journey to the hospital this morning is like one of those nightmares in which you want to run but can't.

It feels like déjà vu as the team wheels Nathaniel in his Isolette—along with the respirator machine, the monitors, and his medications—down the hallway and out the NICU doors. My mom and I follow close behind. At this moment Dr. Smith appears and heads toward me.

"How are you holding up, Christin?" she asks. "I'm sorry to see you under these circumstances, but I can assure you that Nathaniel's in good hands. Dr. Kovalenko will be his surgeon today, and I have complete confidence in his ability to repair the patch. But I'll be on call if he should require any assistance. Do you have any questions?"

I do. "Do you know what caused the patch to come undone?"

"Unfortunately," she says, "there's always a risk of a recurrent hernia, especially when we're dealing with a larger hernia, requiring a patch. It's something we watch for if the baby begins to show signs of distress. I had hoped that this wouldn't be the case for Nathaniel, but I think he should tolerate the surgery well."

"Any idea how long the surgery will last?" I ask as Nathaniel and the team turn the corner and disappear from view.

"I'd estimate five or six hours."

"Okay," I nod with a half smile. "Thank you so much for everything, Dr. Smith."

"My pleasure. Please let me know if you need anything."

As she turns to leave, I'm approached by another nurse.

"You're welcome to wait in Nathaniel's room or the family lounge while Nathaniel's in surgery. Please stay nearby or let us know if you head down to the cafeteria so we can find you if we have any updates."

In the family lounge sit Paul and Harry, two friends that Mau called to pray for us. My mom and I greet them and thank them for coming, letting them know that Nathaniel has just been brought down to the OR.

We all move to the couches and armchairs in the middle of the room, and Harry bows his head. We each take a turn praying for the surgery and for Nathaniel's safety. After the prayer time ends, we send our guests off with hugs and gratitude.

A couple of hours later a nurse enters the lounge.

"I'm happy to report that the surgery is going well," she says. "Nathaniel is much more stable this time around. The surgeon discovered that the seam of the patch broke because Nathaniel grew."

I raise my eyebrows in surprise.

"The surgeon currently has access to the liver; we're wondering if you would give permission for him to do a biopsy to help determine the status of his liver."

"Definitely," I reply without hesitation.

I watch her walk away at a brisk pace, but there's nothing brisk about the passing of time while we wait. Emma alternates between feeding and sleeping as my mom and I continue to pray. The three of us eventually make our way down to the cafeteria for some food, but my stomach is in knots.

On the highway to the north, other vehicles are few and far between, so Mau and his friends take turns testing the car's limits. When riding in the back seat, Mau beseeches the Lord on behalf of his son. The hours on the road give Mau complete awareness of his limitations and helplessness. The situation forces him to exercise his trust in God.

+ + +

At long last the lounge door opens. The clock reads 6:00 p.m.

"I have good news," the nurse says. "Nathaniel is out of surgery, and he's on his way back up to his room as we speak. If you'd like, you can make your way to his room so you're there when he arrives."

"Thank you!" I say. "We'll go right away."

My mom, Emma, and I are waiting when the team shows up with Nathaniel and all his equipment. I can see that he's been reintubated and a new bandage covers the incision site. I step back and dial Mau's phone.

"Honey!" I exclaim. "Nathaniel made it out of surgery, and they just brought him back to his room."

"Praise the Lord! Oh, what a relief!"

Mau says they are about half an hour away. Sure enough, the three travelers arrive on schedule. Mau and I give each other a big hug and heave a sigh of relief—Mau is back, and Nathaniel is stable.

From this point onward, the nurses allow me to enter the NICU with a mask until the feeling in my throat finally goes away. The doctors tell us they're satisfied with Nathaniel's surgery. They were able to replace the patch and drain the fluid that had been preventing his right lung from expanding. Nathaniel is sedated, and the doctors aim to wean him off oxygen and medications once again.

The doctor also shows us an X-ray of Nathaniel's lungs. The left lung now almost completely fills the left side of his chest, but more impressive is the right lung, which has ballooned significantly and now fills about half of the right side. It turns out that the reherniation was a blessing of sorts. By opening Nathaniel up again and draining the excess fluid, they freed his right lung to further expand. This is cause for celebration! What seemed like a devastating step backward has actually been for Nathaniel's good.

We wonder how long it will take for Nathaniel to attain the same progress he reached before the reherniation. We can only hope that the worst is behind us. Only time will tell, and moving forward is the only way.

CHAPTER 14

RAPID PROGRESS

Bless the LORD, O my soul,
and all that is within me,
bless his holy name!
Bless the LORD, O my soul,
and forget not all his benefits,
who forgives all your iniquity,
who heals all your diseases,
who redeems your life from the pit,
who crowns you with steadfast love and mercy.

PSALM 103:1-4

It's been three days since the surgery, and so far, so good. Nathaniel shows no sign of infection and by all accounts is mending well, so I make my own video update. My phone captures a peacefully slumbering Nathaniel. Gone is our puffy, orange, sickly infant. In his place, though he's still skinny, is a baby boy with a normal skin tone. Also, he's been moved to a room with a window that bathes him in glorious sunlight—another sign that he's no longer the same newborn who once required darkness and silence.

Mau's next update reads:

> It's been almost a week since Nathaniel's surgery, and his body seems to be recovering well. The biopsy results of the liver came back showing that the enzyme and bile numbers are decreasing, which is a good sign. There was certainly something there that resolved after the surgery. . . . Let us continue to pray for protection from any infection, for protection of the liver, and for an optimal recovery, especially of the diaphragm that has been repatched. Love you and appreciate you all.

Nathaniel is extubated again, and from this point onward his progress is steady. And I get a long-awaited treat of my own: I have the joy of holding Nathaniel for the first time. A smile lights up my face as I hold him in a tender embrace. He looks so small now that the excess fluid is gone, and at last I'm doing what is natural for every mother to do—holding my child. *Thank You, God! I've been longing for this day, and it's worth the wait.*

I'd always wanted to be a mother. Even though I knew I'd attend university and have a career of some sort, I hoped more than anything that I could one day have children and stay home with them while they were young. Fortunately for me, Mau agreed. The only problem was that when we decided to start trying after three years of marriage, I wasn't able to get pregnant.

The months came and went, but I still wasn't expecting. One day at church I was holding a friend's infant. It was a treat! I was mesmerized watching him gaze upward, enraptured, and I imagined that he could somehow see angels in the rafters. An older lady in the church came over and said with a meaningful wink, "That baby sure looks good on you."

How was I supposed to respond to such a statement? Deep inside, my heart cried out, *I know! Do me a favor, please, and tell God. Maybe He'll listen to you.* Of course, I merely smiled and thanked her.

Infertility is a difficult and lonely road to travel. I saw people around me having babies, and I wondered, *Will it ever be me?* I felt so ready to love and care for a child of my own, yet for reasons beyond my comprehension, it hadn't happened. I grieved a child I had never met, my unfulfilled dream. It's easy to look back and think, *I didn't have to wait all that long.* Which is true. But in the midst of the waiting, I had no idea if or when the situation would ever change. Mau and I continued to pray, not sure of the Lord's will yet hoping that He would give us the gift of a child one day, trusting in His goodness whatever the outcome.

Infertility is a difficult and lonely road to travel. I saw people around me having babies, and I wondered, Will it ever be me?

After a year of trying without success, we were referred to a fertility clinic. We also began to consider the possibility of spending a year in Brazil with Mau's family.

Mau had been living in Canada for eleven years at this point and longed to spend time with his aging parents. Living in Brazil would give me the opportunity to improve my Portuguese, and we could still pursue options to grow our family from there. At the same time, Mau felt a growing call from the Lord to pursue full-time Christian ministry.

After some prayer we decided to make the trip. We found some trusted friends to rent our house, our employers handled our resignations with grace and sent us with their blessing, and we had some job prospects lined up in Brazil. Everything seemed to be coming together. And then something wonderfully unexpected happened: I discovered that I was pregnant.

It was November 2012. We had just moved out of our house and were staying with some friends before heading to Brazil when I had a hunch. Mau and I had to make a trip to the supermarket, and I wanted to surprise him, so I bought a pregnancy test and a *You're the Best Dad* greeting card without him noticing. That simple test confirmed my suspicion.

"Mau, I've got something for you," I said later that evening. I handed him the card, unable to hide my excitement.

With a puzzled expression, he took the card and opened it. I had changed the card to read *You're* Going to Be *the Best Dad*. His puzzled expression deepened; then the meaning of the card slowly crystallized.

"What?" he wondered.

"I'm pregnant!" I cried with glee.

Mau was dumbfounded. His mind was still processing the news that I'd already had time to digest. When he was finally able to respond, he said, "This is incredible, but what do we do now? I mean, we just quit our jobs and packed up all our things. How are we going to do this?"

Not quite the response I had expected, but still understandable.

We certainly did have a dilemma. Should we still go to Brazil, or should we do the responsible thing—try to get our jobs back while we still could and prepare for the baby? Yet as we thought and prayed about it, we decided to take a step of faith and continue with our travel plans.

In the end we flew to Brazil and spent six months with Mau's family. We were able to share with them the joyful anticipation of new life as we watched my belly grow—a blessing we'd have never known if we'd been apart. We flew back to Canada in May 2013, two months before my due date, and stayed with my parents in Edmonton until we could move back into our home after our rental agreement ended. It was another beautiful opportunity for family members—this time mine—to join in our delight as we welcomed little Thomas into the world on July 21, 2013. (He was born at the same hospital I was.)

When Thomas was born I fretted needlessly about naps, bedtime routines, and sleeping through the night. Given that he was my one and only responsibility, coupled with my perfectionistic personality, I expected things to go the way the books said they should. Moreover, I was frustrated and perplexed if they didn't. With time, however, I found my parenting footing and learned to relax a bit. I was enjoying my role as a first-time mom.

Now I am cradling Nathaniel for the first time and also giving him his first bottle, which contains a small amount of my breast milk. He tires of feeding after a short time, so the nurse gives him the remaining milk through his feeding tube. We'll keep at this daily feeding because it's an important skill for him to learn before he can be released.

The following afternoon the doctor on shift comes to Nathaniel's room. Mau has just arrived from work.

"Let me update you on Nathaniel's current status," the doctor says. "We've begun decreasing the dosage of medications, and last night he was quite uncomfortable from withdrawal. Today he's been quite calm though."

"I'm glad to hear he's had a better day," I say.

She continues, "His big challenge at this point is putting on weight. He's only just returned to his birth weight, which isn't surprising given that in seven weeks he underwent two surgeries and hasn't been able to feed and grow like a normal, healthy baby."

I glance toward Nathaniel, who has grown longer since he was born but now has the look of a somewhat malnourished child.

"We've been trying to feed him high-caloric formula to augment the nutrition he's receiving, but because of his stomach sensitivity we've only been able to give him breast milk. Normally breast milk would be sufficient, but since you don't have a large supply"—remember, I am also nursing his sister!—"we've had to access donated milk. When donated milk is pasteurized and frozen, it unfortunately loses almost all its nutrients. We're hoping that Nathaniel will soon be able to tolerate formula, which will speed up his recovery so he can go home."

Home? When did we reach the point where going home is now part of the conversation? Home still seems so far off, like a distant galaxy viewed through the lens of a telescope.

"When do you think he'll be ready to go home?" Mau asks.

"He should be ready in another four weeks or so, once his breathing has improved and he's gained some weight."

Mau and I are grateful for the positive update, but as always, we still send another prayer request to our network in response to these latest needs.

The hospital has become like home over these past several weeks. I've met most of the doctors and nurses, and I've also experienced the kindness of the cleaning staff. They have given Nathaniel and the other NICU patients little gifts, like booties and stuffed animals, but there's one woman in particular who stands out. There's something special about her—a gentle peace and love radiate from her. Every time she enters Nathaniel's room, even if it's simply to empty the garbage, she says hello with a smile. Over time we get to know one another. I learn that she has immigrated from Africa and is a Christian.

"I love the babies here," she tells me. "As I clean each room, I pray for them."

I'm surprised and touched to discover that a prayer warrior walks these halls and lifts the children up in prayer.

We're also surprised when Nathaniel receives an anonymous gift. It's a toy that plays music to accompany an undersea scene filled with moving sea creatures. We attach it to Nathaniel's crib, and it provides welcome stimulation for a boy who is still largely restricted to his bed. He stares at it wide-eyed, eyebrows raised, mouth gaping, mesmerized as the music plays and a crab, octopus, and clown fish dance on a screen lit by blue light. We joke that he has his own personal TV—Thomas will be jealous!

On May 13 the doctors move Nathaniel to a less invasive breathing support system. I get to hold him for some much-needed kangaroo care, and I now have a clear view of his angelic face. I suspect that he's enjoying the greater visibility and freedom to move, especially as he watches his new TV.

Mau visits after work and composes an enthusiastic update:

> Hey, guys, thank you for your prayers! We're grateful to the Lord that Nathaniel is getting better every day! He's breathing a lot on his own and is getting better! . . . Please continue to pray that Nathaniel will gain weight and learn to bottle-feed. Let's pray for his liver as well. His skin color is better, but his eyes still show that his liver is not 100 percent.
>
> Christin has had the opportunity to spend more time at the hospital, which has provided opportunities for nurses and other families to witness God's grace, power, and peace in us and for us. We don't know how much longer we will be there, so please pray with us that God will work out His purposes.

I'm quite taken aback by Nathaniel's progress; he is improving with a speed I never imagined possible. Our fear of a second infection hasn't materialized, and the doctors are telling us again that he's doing better than expected, moving from fragility and reliance toward strength and independence.

+ + +

Little Greyson's journey is a far different story. While Nathaniel is making steady improvement, Greyson is not. While Nathaniel is breathing almost entirely on his own, Greyson remains fully intubated. While Nathaniel enjoys a room filled with sunlight, Greyson remains in the darkness of the CDH wing. While the doctors speak to us of home, they speak to Melissa of palliative care. We're filled with joy. She's filled with anger. Like us, she's unwilling to give up on her son. Holding on to any glimmer of hope, no matter how small, she's determined to fight for her son until there's no fight left.

"They want to take him off the ventilator!" Melissa explodes, hands clenched in fists, when Mau and I speak with her. "I'm not ready to do that! He still has life in him—I can't let him go."

I don't know what to say to comfort her, but I whisper a silent prayer and wonder, *Why is Nathaniel getting better but not Greyson?*

"They want to take him off the ventilator!" Melissa explodes, hands clenched in fists.

Mau has ministered to Melissa faithfully over the past two months. He or one of our pastors has prayed with her and Greyson virtually every day, and Mau has encouraged her, calmed her, and offered support. He does so again today.

+ + +

We make our way to the hospital after church, Thomas with us. It's May 21, Mau's birthday, but any special plans are an afterthought with so much else going on. Nathaniel is asleep in his bed, wrapped snugly in the same turquoise blanket that Mauricio's great-great-grandma knit for him when he was a baby.

"Hey, buddy," Mau whispers to his sleeping child.

Mau lifts Thomas up to take a look at his little brother. Amber is taking care of Nathaniel today. "Do you notice anything?" she says to us.

"Oh my goodness!" Mau exclaims. "Look—he's breathing on his own! The nasal prongs are gone!"

"What?" I'm stunned. "No way!"

It's true. There he is, all breathing support gone. Just two months after being born with minuscule lungs, here he is breathing on his own. I was so focused on the challenge of just surviving. Now I feel like we've won the lottery.

"I couldn't have asked for a better birthday present!" Mau says. "God, You are so good, so faithful."

Mau's message to our friends and family today is short and sweet:

He's off all artificial breathing support. What a birthday present!

Three days later I'm in Nathaniel's room with Emma, making a video of the two of them, when I suddenly gasp. *Nathaniel smiled! His first smile!* My heart swells as I gaze at his darling face. Eyes fixed on me. Lips curved up. Mouth slightly open. Pink tongue showing.

Happy.

Mau sends a new update:

Hi, everyone! Nathaniel is an active and normal baby who now demands more attention and time. . . . The nurses have nothing much else to do but feed him. The doctors said yesterday he might come home next week! Let's see—we're not in a hurry.

A day or two later the doctors tell us that he's ready to go home. Mau and I are taken aback. I thought he would stay for at least a couple more weeks.

"Are you sure he's ready?" I ask.

"Yes, we are. He's been weaned off most of his medications, he's feeding well, and we're sure you'll be able to care for him at home."

"But wouldn't it be better if he stayed here just to make sure he's okay?" Mau asks.

We're both a bit overwhelmed, unsure that we're ready to take on the responsibility of Nathaniel's care. He's such a skinny, floppy little guy, and he still seems so weak—are we really capable of caring for him on our own? *What if he doesn't gain weight? He won't be attached to monitors, so how will we know if he's getting enough oxygen? Will I be able to give him his medications properly? And what about his feeding tube? He still can't take a whole bottle without tiring out.*

The doctor sees the insecurity on our faces. "We find that most babies do very well once they go home," she says. "When babies like Nathaniel are surrounded by the love of their families and engage in normal interactions, they usually thrive and gain more weight than they would in the hospital. There isn't much else we can do for him here. You don't need to worry—we'll show you everything you need to know before he goes home."

It takes us another day to conclude that we're okay with it. I'm the first to realize the benefits of having Nathaniel at home. No longer will I feel torn about neglecting one or more of my children—we'll all be together at last. The thought of having the freedom to remain home all day together—without needing to pack everyone up, drop Thomas off here or there, and troop back home again—sounds like a wish come true. Best of all, it means that Nathaniel will no longer be separated from the family who loves him so very much. Mau comes to the same conclusion and, like flipping a switch, the medical staff begin to prepare us to bring our boy home.

What a journey this has been! We've gone from standing vigil over a critically ill newborn, silent and still, to holding an alert and curious infant who has learned to smile and is finding his voice after weeks of being intubated.

We witness our first hint of our little guy's personality on May 29. Mau, Emma, and I are in the hospital room together, and Nathaniel is in my lap looking up at me. I talk with him the same way we've interacted with Emma since her birth, and I'm astounded when I'm rewarded with the most radiant baby smile I've ever seen. This moment brings with it the realization that Nathaniel is no longer the sick baby he once was but a "real" boy—a boy with a big heart and the capacity to give and receive love.

"Hello!" I say and erupt with giggles at the sight of his glowing face. "Mau, look at him!" I don't want Mau to miss this marvel. "Aww, you're so cute! That's the biggest smile I've ever seen," I coo. "We can't wait for you to come home, Mr. Smiley Boy."

Despite everything this little boy has gone through, he's joyful. It's like he's wired for joy. Despite the pain and suffering, Nathaniel has made it through the fire. Those who would argue that Nathaniel's life should have been snuffed out in order to spare either him or us, his parents, from suffering are mistaken and shortsighted. Yes, he has suffered tremendous pain; and yes, we have endured an arduous journey; but we would do it all over again to come out on the other side graced with our son's beautiful smile.

We would also do it all over again even if the outcome had gone the other way. We'd be grateful to have met our son and to have loved him for every moment we were given. We wouldn't regret giving him the blessing of birth and a chance for life. Despite his skinny limbs and lean face, God has blessed Nathaniel with a cheerful heart.

Our joy-filled boy is ready to come home, and we're ready to receive him. Taking on the responsibility of his care will be a challenge, but I'm eager for him to bond with Thomas and Emma—our family time has been incomplete without his presence. I'm definitely nervous, but I'm also ready to bring our sweet boy home. Let's do this!

CHAPTER 15

THERE'S NO PLACE LIKE HOME

"Do not be anxious about tomorrow, for tomorrow will be anxious for itself. Sufficient for the day is its own trouble."

MATTHEW 6:34

In preparation for Nathaniel's homecoming, I decide he needs some special going-home garb to mark the occasion. I search the store racks looking for just the right ensemble—a cute denim one-piece outfit covered in little blue elephants.

We also prepare things at home. We get the bassinet ready for Nathaniel, and I buy a bunch of new bottles because I'll soon need to accommodate both babies. And, of course, the second car seat waits at the ready.

I remember how cavernous this place felt to us after starting out in a tiny apartment. The kitchen cabinets were ample, the empty basement perfect for floor hockey. I remember envisioning our future family filling its rooms—kids playing in the backyard, toys strewn about on the floor. Now the place feels like an overstuffed suitcase, but I wouldn't change it for the world.

The most important skill I still have to learn is how to insert Nathaniel's feeding tube. Although his strength continues to grow, he isn't quite able to take an entire bottle at each feeding. Whatever he can't finish, along with the two or three medications he's still on, must be given through his tube.

Before we know the exact day Nathaniel will come home, his nurse tells me it's time I learn to do it.

"Okay, if you say so," I reply, biting my lip and raising an uncertain eyebrow.

Though I'm terrified inside, I try not to show it. The nurse shows me the steps, and I'm somehow able to replicate them successfully. The nurse gives me written instructions in case I forget what to do while I hope and pray I won't have to do this again at home. *I'm not cut out to be a nurse,* I determine.

On May 30 the doctor on shift tells me that the time has come: Nathaniel is ready to go home, he says. Tomorrow.

"Tomorrow?" I ask, still disbelieving.

"Tomorrow," he replies with a smile. "But in order to do that, you'll need to stay overnight with Nathaniel and manage his care on your own. We'll unhook all the monitors and let him sleep as he would at home. We'll wake him for his feedings every three hours as usual, which you'll give him, and we'll see how it goes. I'm sure you'll both do great."

I glance down at Emma in my arms. "Should I keep Emma with me tonight too?" I ask.

"I think it'd be best if she stays with your husband. It'll be important for you to spend this time with Nathaniel without any distractions."

"I can't believe this is actually happening," I reply.

The doctor proceeds to list a host of concerns to watch out for, including gastroesophageal reflux, RSV, pneumonia, insufficient growth, and even hearing loss.

The doctor finally pauses. "Do you have any questions?"

My mind is swimming with all this information, and I wonder how I'll ever be able to keep track of it all.

"You can always call us here if you have any concerns."

That makes me feel better, but only marginally. This all feels daunting. It's reassuring, at least, to know that Nathaniel's health will be monitored and we won't be all alone in the weeks to come. When I think the doctor can't possibly have anything else to share, I'm mistaken.

"In addition, Nathaniel will come to the CDH clinic every three months for the first year, then annually afterward until he's sixteen. We'll also arrange for Nathaniel to see a cardiologist, who will track his pulmonary hypertension for the next several years."

Oh boy. This is too much. Deep breath in, deep breath out.

"I know this is a lot to take in," he says, noticing my panicked expression. "Please don't worry. We wouldn't be sending Nathaniel home if we didn't think both he and you were ready."

"Okay," I reply. "If you say so."

I call Mau and share the news. Like me, he is excited but nervous. I'll head home with Emma late that afternoon, pick Thomas up from my parents' house on the way, and meet Mau at the house. I'll pack my overnight bag, make sure Mau has everything he needs for feeding Emma that night, eat a quick meal, and return to the hospital.

A nurse prepares a schedule for me so that I can keep track of everything from feedings to medications to pumping breast milk. She also gives me a number of printouts filled with information about what to look out for and who to call if Nathaniel's health takes a turn for the worse.

My heart rate accelerates. Panic rises as my stomach clenches. *How will I be able to take care of all three kids—especially Nathaniel, who needs so much extra care? What if something goes wrong with him? Will I be able to handle an emergency? What if Mau isn't home and something happens? Lord, please help me.*

I decide that my daily goal, plain and simple, is survival. I just have to take one day at a time, recognizing that the Lord will give me strength for that day. If I focus on the magnitude of the entire task ahead, I'll be overcome by the enormity of it all; but if I take a step-by-step approach, I'm sure I'll make it through.

I remind myself what Jesus taught about worry:

> "Therefore I tell you, do not be anxious about your life, what you will eat or what you will drink, nor about your body, what you will put on. Is not life more than food, and the body more than clothing? . . . And which of you by being anxious can add a single hour to his span of life? . . .
>
> "Therefore do not be anxious about tomorrow, for tomorrow will be anxious for itself. Sufficient for the day is its own trouble."
>
> MATTHEW 6:25, 27, 34

I can only imagine the weight I'll carry in the days to come, but I know that the Lord has brought us this far and is not about to desert us now.

I return to the hospital that evening. For the first time since the twins were born, I can give Nathaniel my undivided attention. I relax as I cradle my baby, thankful that tonight I don't have to leave him. At seven o'clock the lights in the NICU dim, and my little guy soon falls asleep. I drift off on the couch just a few feet away. The night goes off without a hitch, and before I know it, we awake to a promising new day.

I can only imagine the weight I'll carry in the days to come, but I know that the Lord has brought us this far and is not about to desert us now.

Everyone who enters Nathaniel's room greets us with knowing smiles. This is the day we've anticipated for months, the way one yearns for the return of a loved one who's been away for far too long.

The regularly updated whiteboard in Nathaniel's room reads much like it does on any other day:

Today's Date: May 31, 2017
I Like to Be Called: Nathaniel
My Important People:
Dad: Mauricio
Mom: Christin
Big Brother: Thomas
Twin Sister: Emma
I Like: cuddles, my soother, Mommy's milk, my TV
My Nurse: Kelly

MY CARE TEAM:
Neonatologist: Dr. West
Charge Nurse: Carol

But today there is one significant difference:

PLANS: **Go home today!**

I have to pinch myself to believe that this day has come. A mere ten weeks after birth—ten weeks of valiant battle and great endurance—Nathaniel is ready to begin the next chapter of his life.

Mau arrives at the hospital with Emma midmorning. The second car seat we rushed to buy the day of the twins' birth is ready to go. We pack up supplies, receive final instructions, and accept congratulations from well-wishers. At last we sign the discharge papers.

It's official: Nathaniel is free to leave.

+ + +

After facilitating the program for immigrant mothers for two years, I had settled into a comfortable routine. Every six months my teammates and I welcomed a new group of women from all over the world. I never tired of hearing their stories and learning about their cultures. Occasionally I even got to meet their children.

One day in class our discussion veered off topic, and I shared my pro-life views. The following week a client stayed after class to speak with me.

"Last week," she shared, "I was scheduled to have an abortion.

I'd gone for the first appointment, and I was supposed to go back on Friday. That's when they were going to do it."

I looked at her in surprise, waiting for her to continue.

"But after what you said in class," she said, "I changed my mind. I just couldn't go through with it."

I stood there speechless. I thought of her six-year-old daughter and her supportive husband. "But why were you going to have an abortion?" I asked. "I'm so thankful you didn't, but I don't understand."

"I didn't want having another baby to interfere with my career plans."

Ohhh . . . A weight of sadness accompanied my realization. We had just spent weeks researching careers and schooling to help these women develop five-year action plans for restarting their careers in Canada. The idea that someone might abort their baby to fulfill their plan had never entered my mind. Perhaps she felt she had no choice because our program would track the outcomes of our clients once they graduated.

"It's just a career plan," I told her, "and plans change. Maybe you'll have to put things on hold for a while, but that's okay—it'll be there waiting for you when you're ready."

I thought about my own desire to have a baby. "There's nothing more important than your family. And by the way, congratulations! I'm so happy for you!"

We laughed together, and she seemed relieved. So was I. *Thank You, Lord! If You hadn't orchestrated that discussion, her baby might have been lost.*

Our conversation was a wake-up call. I didn't want to be involved in unwittingly encouraging young women to choose their careers over children; I soon moved to a different role in the organization.

Like Nathaniel, another baby was free to live her life as God intended and with a mom free from the pain of regret.

+ + +

We make sure to say goodbye to Amber, Nathaniel's nurse and greatest cheerleader—a woman who has earned a special place in our hearts. She hands me a plastic bag filled with mementos from Nathaniel's long stay. There's a plastic vial with a few wisps of hair retrieved after his first unwanted but necessary haircut, a card with the silver imprint of his tiny foot, the colorful nametag that labeled his room, identification wristbands, and a few photographs.

The most remarkable item is the long strand of his Beads of Courage. Measuring about fifteen feet in length, the many glass beads of various shapes and colors join together in a vibrant procession. Each bead type represents a specific challenge or procedure Nathaniel faced: black for every poke, yellow for each day of his hospital stay, and purple for the completion of a treatment. For years to come, we'll look at these beads and say, "Nathaniel, look at everything you overcame. The Lord was with you then, He's with you now, and He'll be with you forever."

I dress Nathaniel in his going-home outfit. The poor guy is so scrawny that folds of fabric envelop him. Amber takes family photos with Mau's phone. Little Nathaniel's head is slumped to one side, with a tube taped to his cheek and a hand concealed inside his voluminous sleeve. Emma, on the other hand, holds her head up with ease, visibly longer, rosier, and plumper than her twin brother.

Viewing the twins side by side paints a picture of stark differences. I can't help but feel sorry for Nathaniel. It seems unfair that Nathaniel's struggle has left him pale, malnourished, and limp while Emma is a picture of health. But it is what it is. His lengthy hospital stay was the only way for Nathaniel to be here with us today, alive and—all things considered—well. This current season of physical weakness will one day pass.

The poor guy is so scrawny that folds of fabric envelop him.

Amber joins us in the family lounge for the last time. We buckle Nathaniel into his new car seat and cover him with his special blue blanket, then repeat the process with Emma. The twins are reunited at last, ready for their first stroller ride and car trip together. Amber takes another picture of us, Mau and I smiling beside the two babies.

I thank Amber for everything.

"You're so welcome!" she replies. "Nathaniel is a special little guy, and I'm so happy he's going home. We'll miss him!"

We wave one final goodbye and head out the double doors of the NICU for the last time. This is it. Nathaniel is leaving the hospital. He's going home.

It's beginning to sink in—Nathaniel has made it! It also hits me that God has answered all three of our initial prayers—my parents moved to Calgary, the twins made it to thirty-eight weeks, and God saved Nathaniel's life.

I don't know why God has chosen to let us take Nathaniel home when so many other babies have moved on to their heavenly home. I just don't know. There's certainly nothing special about us, and I grieve with those who have lost children. Though I often don't understand, I must leave outcomes in God's hands. When things go well and when they don't, when I rejoice and when I mourn, He remains Lord of all.

Psalm 34:17-18 beautifully expresses both situations:

> When the righteous cry for help, the LORD hears
> and delivers them out of all their troubles.
> The LORD is near to the brokenhearted
> and saves the crushed in spirit.

The Lord hears our cries, and He is near when our hearts break. My soul rejoices as I meditate on these verses. What a wild ride this has been!

PART THREE

"Where's My Happy Ending?"

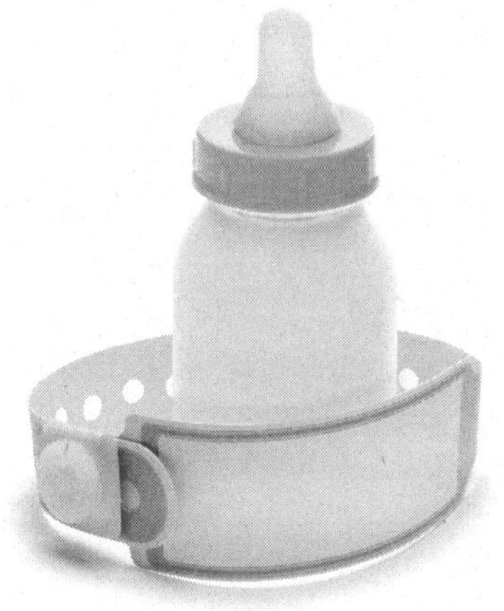

CHAPTER 16

MAKING SENSE OF IT ALL

"I sewed myself a shroud and wore it like a shirt;
I lay facedown in the dirt.
Now my face is blotched red from weeping;
look at the dark shadows under my eyes,
Even though I've never hurt a soul
and my prayers are sincere!"

JOB 16:15–17, MSG

The day after we arrive home, we receive the news: Greyson has passed away. After months of intubation, his little lungs give out, no longer able to perform their function. He has breathed his last breath and his soul is at peace, yet his parents grieve. They are filled with anguish, hearts torn in two, emotions in turmoil. I can only imagine what they must be thinking: *Why did Greyson have to die?*

Our hearts break for them. Words can't convey our sadness and how we wish the outcome could have been different.

Mau is once again there when Melissa needs him. She has no

idea where to turn or what to do, so Mau directs her to a funeral home that helps her make the necessary arrangements. She reconnects with our pastor, who offers to speak at the memorial service, and Mau takes charge of planning the food and flowers.

Melissa and I exchange texts. I ask how she's been holding up; her reply is honest and filled with grief. She asks how our kids are doing; my reply is also honest—they're happy and bonding with Nathaniel. She texts back that she's "jealous-happy" for me, which is completely understandable. This conversation isn't easy for either of us. What can I say to comfort someone when I have the very thing she's lost? Why were *we* the ones to bring home a healthy child? Where is God in all this?

Is there anger mixed with her sadness? Is she somehow making sense of this great loss?

Greyson's memorial service begins with a procession of six people, me included, each of us a few feet apart holding a seemingly endless Beads of Courage strand with hundreds of beads. The strand stretches out for at least twenty feet, each bead representing one of the many procedures Greyson endured during his abbreviated life. This visual representation of his tenacity is both a sobering and an honoring tribute.

Then Melissa and her husband, a quiet man, make their way to the front. As the pair stand side by side, Melissa shares a stirring eulogy chronicling the details of Greyson's life and the gratitude they feel for every moment they were blessed to spend with him. Our pastor concludes the service with words of hope for a family unfamiliar with the only true hope that is found in Jesus.

Over the following weeks Melissa and I continue to correspond by text, though the messages become increasingly sporadic.

Months later, after several failed attempts to connect in person, Melissa expresses her ongoing struggles with grief and trauma—the unwelcome byproducts of all she has borne. I wonder what thoughts might be plaguing her. Is there anger mixed with her sadness? Is she somehow making sense of this great loss? Has she found any peace or comfort?

Perhaps you, too, are grieving the loss of a baby. Or perhaps your preborn child has received a life-limiting prenatal diagnosis. Perhaps you're currently questioning the goodness of God. If that's you, first let me say that I'm truly sorry for the pain you've endured. In the midst of your heartbreak, I encourage you to continue reading and to let the Lord's words of comfort and solace be a balm for your soul as we consider the question of your suffering.

In the following chapters you'll read the stories of two couples who have suffered. Their stories are marked with loss and lament. They didn't get happy endings. You'll hear about how God was with them on their journeys, comforting and consoling them each step of the way, drawing them to Himself, and teaching them hard-earned lessons of tremendous worth.

CHAPTER 17

THIAGO AND KARYNNE'S STORY

We know that for those who love God all things work together for good, for those who are called according to his purpose.

ROMANS 8:28

Mau and I met Thiago and Karynne several years ago when they joined our church after immigrating from Brazil. Like Mau and me, they were experiencing infertility, and they used the same IUI treatment that we would employ just a few months later. Eight weeks into her pregnancy, Karynne began bleeding—a lot. She went to the ER, had an ultrasound, and was told that everything was fine. Much to her amazement, the couple also learned that they were expecting twins!

This being her first pregnancy, Karynne wasn't sure what was normal, yet to her things just didn't feel right. The bleeding returned, so she went back to the ER, was checked out, and was again sent home. She ran the same drill several more times. Again and again the bleeding came back, and each time she was assured that the babies were well. Despite these assurances, Karynne wondered if the Lord was preparing her for something—though for what she wasn't sure.

Karynne was twenty-three weeks along when she returned to the hospital one more time. This time the doctor determined that her cervix was soft, so she was admitted to the hospital to be monitored. Within the next few hours, she was already beginning to dilate.

At this point everything changed. The babies would be arriving early—of this there was no doubt. Alone at this late hour without the support of her husband (Thiago hadn't been allowed to stay overnight), Karynne was told there was an 80-percent chance that the babies wouldn't make it—and if they did survive, there was a 40-percent chance they would have developmental difficulties like blindness, brain damage, cognitive delays, and hearing loss. Rather than crumple in fear at this dismal prognosis, she felt the peace of God in that moment—the peace that surpasses all understanding—and fell back asleep.

By morning Thiago was at Karynne's side. They were inundated with statistics about infant mortality and long-term complications, and they had to sign multiple forms and waivers in preparation for the twins' birth. They were asked by numerous doctors if they wanted to continue with the pregnancy but were never pressured to have an abortion. Though the couple was resolute in their decision to fight for their babies and assured that the twins would receive lifesaving care, if they hadn't already had a firm foundation in Christ, it would have been easy to be influenced in a different direction.

At twenty-three weeks and six days, one of the placentas ruptured, and that baby's vitals started showing signs of distress.

Karynne was rushed into an OR filled with a staggering nineteen people for an emergency C-section. Her twin girls were delivered just after midnight on August 23, 2016. Baby Deborah survived and was rushed to the NICU; baby Acsa did not make it.

These first-time parents struggled to manage their conflicting emotions—extraordinary joy over one baby's survival competed with unrelenting sorrow over the loss of the other. They also had to contend with the doctors' pronouncement that tiny Deborah would likely experience developmental problems and would live a life of dependency. When Karynne went home for the first time after the babies' birth, it was in an empty car devoid of the soft sounds of newborns. She wept a tidal wave of tears.

At this point in the story, you might be asking yourself, *What did they do to deserve this outcome? It's so unfair!* Yet before reaching this conclusion, take a step back to consider what the Bible teaches us starting at the beginning, in the second and third chapters of Genesis. God has just finished creating the earth and all that is in it. Adam and Eve are enjoying an idyllic life in the Garden of Eden, and the Lord has instructed them that they can eat from any tree in the Garden except for the tree of the knowledge of good and evil, for if they do, then they will surely die.

These first-time parents struggled to manage their conflicting emotions—extraordinary joy over one baby's survival competed with unrelenting sorrow over the loss of the other.

Obeying that one rule should be no problem, right? Wrong. Eve is deceived and eats the forbidden fruit. She then offers it to Adam, who also takes a bite. They have sinned against God, and suddenly the perfect world He created is forever changed—marred and broken by the effects of sin. The couple is banished from the Garden, their innocence lost and their perfect communion with God ruined. They will now experience pain and heavy toil until the day they die. And every person since—including you and me—is born with a sinful nature into a world ravaged by sin. Adam and Eve's own son Cain becomes the first murderer when he kills his brother.

What does this mean for us, and for parents who lose a precious child? It means we shouldn't be surprised when hard times come. No one is immune to the effects of living in a sinful world filled with people capable of committing acts of unspeakable evil. If we're honest with ourselves, we can admit that we sometimes make choices that hurt both ourselves and others. Thus everyone will suffer at some point in life. As Christian author and pastor Tim Keller aptly puts it, "Perhaps the real puzzle is this: Why, in light of our behavior as a human race, does God allow so much *happiness*?"[1]

But I'm a good person, you might say. *I lead a good life; I treat people well; I'm not a murderer or a thief or a pedophile. Why should bad things happen to me? Hasn't God promised to protect me from harm?* While it's true that the Bible teaches that there are logical consequences to our actions—Proverbs is chock-full of such wisdom: The righteous will succeed, but the wicked will come to ruin; hard work leads to wealth, but laziness leads to poverty—oftentimes even relatively good people suffer.

Look at the story of Job. He's a God-honoring man with no apparent faults (see Job 29 for a description of his many good deeds), yet for no humanly discernible reason, disaster befalls him. He loses his fortune, his children die in a terrible accident, and he's tormented by painful sores that cover his body. *It doesn't make sense. It isn't fair.* But in light of our broken world—a world where sickness can strike no matter how healthy one's lifestyle, a world where hard work doesn't always pay off, a world where bad things can happen through no fault of one's own—good people like Job *can* and *do* suffer.

Yet Job will not curse God, even though he knows he's apparently done nothing to deserve this cataclysmic turn of events. Job pours out his lament to God, questioning Him in great agony and even cursing the day of his birth—yet he never curses God. When the Lord finally responds, He doesn't explain His reasons for letting Job suffer, but instead He questions Job. For four chapters He asks questions such as these: "Where were you when I laid the foundation of the earth? . . . Have you commanded the morning since your days began, and caused the dawn to know its place? . . . Have you entered into the springs of the sea, or walked in the recesses of the deep?" (Job 38:4, 12, 16).

These questions go on as Job is thoroughly put in his place by his Creator. His complaints are silenced in the presence of God. Job is a seemingly innocent man who nonetheless endures great suffering. It doesn't seem fair. Yet he acknowledges that God is sovereign. Is this the end of the discussion?

Thiago and Karynne were in that place—seemingly good people who suffered nonetheless, facing the greatest test to their faith they had ever encountered. How would they respond? One daughter was fighting for her life with the very real likelihood of long-term disability; the other's fight was already over. Would they curse God and throw in the towel, or would they continue to trust His divine will for their lives?

With family, friends, and church members praying for and supporting them, and with a firm belief in the goodness of God, Thiago and Karynne never raged at God. Nor did they question why or how this tragedy could have befallen them. From the very first sign of trouble, despite their fears and insecurities, they voiced their trust in God. They recognized that He would do as He pleased, and they chose to accept His decision.

If God wanted both girls to survive and live normal lives, amen. If He decided to take one and not the other, or even take both, amen. Thiago and Karynne declared with their mouths that the Lord was in control and that the impossible belonged to Him. Once they placed their fears in Jesus' capable hands, they felt the peace of Christ settle over them.

In faith they prayed for Deborah, who surprised the doctors as she beat the odds. In sadness they planned a memorial service for Acsa. When a hospital social worker came to see how Karynne was faring, Karynne told her that she and Thiago were well because God was with them, strengthening them. Even the nurses commented on Karynne's happiness and how her faith was helping her.

How could they have that kind of response? How could they be so calm after losing one child and knowing that the other might not make it either? Thiago explained it to me like this:

> God is sovereign—if God is leading you through this journey, He has a purpose. He's good, and His will is perfect and good despite the hardship. That was our foundation. We never made decisions based on feelings. Like Job said, God gives and takes away; we honor Him regardless. Acsa is part of the family. We talk about her, and we know exactly where she is.

Jesus makes all the difference. Jesus—God's precious Son—left the infinite glory of heaven to be born into a humble family, to live a humble life, and to die an excruciating death even though He was faultless. He died for *our* sins; He suffered to save *us*. It says in Isaiah 53:3, 5:

> He was despised and rejected by men,
> a man of sorrows and acquainted with grief. . . .
> But he was pierced for our transgressions;
> he was crushed for our iniquities;
> upon him was the chastisement that brought us peace,
> and with his wounds we are healed.

Is there anything more convincing than Jesus' sacrifice to prove that God loves us? Jesus can relate to our pain—He's been there. He can relate to our sorrow—He's felt it. He can commiserate with our rejection—He's experienced it. All for love. Love for us. To reconcile us to the Father. An innocent man who nonetheless endured great suffering. It didn't seem fair. Yet He knew the Father is sovereign.

For Thiago and Karynne, though they don't know why God chose to take Acsa, they do know that her life had value and she fulfilled her purpose by drawing others closer to Jesus. And God has used Deborah, who was able to leave the hospital after ninety-five days and has enjoyed good health ever since, to show how He is able to do more than we could ever possibly imagine.

But what about those whose children—or who themselves—suffer with long-term physical or cognitive disabilities? How is God working together all things for good when your child endures major health problems and your family has to hold up under stress that never seems to end? Let's take a look at another family's journey.

CHAPTER 18

GLENN AND CATHERINE'S STORY

Count it all joy, my brothers, when you meet trials of various kinds, for you know that the testing of your faith produces steadfastness. And let steadfastness have its full effect, that you may be perfect and complete, lacking in nothing.

JAMES 1:2-4

Catherine has been a good friend of mine since high school, and she hasn't changed very much over the years. Sure, she's a doctor and is married with three kids now, but she hasn't lost her zest for life, her infectious laugh, or her love for Jesus. The most amazing thing is that her faith remains strong despite her familiarity with hardship.

After three years of infertility, Catherine and her husband, Glenn, found out they were expecting. An ultrasound at twelve weeks suggested there could be problems, and later testing showed that their child had major heart abnormalities—life-threatening but operable. At six days old, baby Josiah had his first surgery. Everything seemed to have gone well at first, but when the doctors discovered internal bleeding, they had to operate again. Then, much like Nathaniel, Josiah contracted an infection that kept him in the hospital six weeks longer than they had anticipated.

Then came the day when Josiah was finally discharged. Assuming her son was out of the woods, Catherine hung around to distribute cards to the NICU moms she'd met before heading home with her son. On their way out of the hospital, Josiah in his stroller, Catherine pushing from behind, the nurses noticed that the boy was blue, grabbed him out of his stroller, and rushed him back into the hospital for intubation.

Catherine was shaken to the core: If she hadn't handed out those cards—if she'd left just ten minutes earlier—she might have arrived home with a dead child. It was after this brush with death that Catherine realized her parenting journey might never be normal.

Several weeks and many tests later, Josiah was once again discharged, this time with plans for more cardiac interventions. Sent home with a feeding tube because he was too weak to drink from a bottle, Josiah also struggled with oral aversion and retching. He made another trip to the ICU for aspiration pneumonia and had a tube surgically inserted that allowed formula to be pumped directly into his stomach.

It was after this brush with death that Catherine realized her parenting journey might never be normal.

While that tube helped Josiah get the nutrition he needed, his heart was still weak and failing, requiring frequent trips to the hospital and countless appointments with specialists. He received multiple stents to alleviate pulmonary hypertension and eventually needed an additional open-heart surgery. Leading up to the surgery, then-six-year-old Josiah experienced a catastrophic trip to the catheterization lab, where he went into respiratory distress due to a virus. The virus that first manifested in his lungs went on to attack his brain, which left him unable to walk for a time. Adding to the chaos during this time, Glenn and Catherine welcomed two more children to their family. Let's just say that life wasn't easy.

Thankfully, Josiah enjoyed substantial improvement after the ordeal of his second heart surgery. Instead of worrying about whether their son would need a heart transplant, Glenn and Catherine were able to focus on Josiah's non-life-threatening issues, such as a paralyzed vocal cord, developmental delays, and ongoing oral aversion and refusal to take food by mouth. At seven years of age, he participated in a special weeks-long feeding clinic. And it worked! After a nightmarish seven years, Glenn and Catherine now had a different child. His successful surgery combined with regular eating did wonders to strengthen Josiah's heart.

Today Josiah is in junior high school and doing better than his parents, physicians, and therapists ever predicted. Though he carries permanent physical and emotional scars and faces a lifetime of medical testing, procedures, and surgeries, some hope has been restored.

"God is not defined or limited by what the doctors, psychologists, and tests show," Catherine says. "And we don't want our kids defined by that either. God has plans for them, and He will use the hardships they face for His glory and for their long-term good."

"We have experienced God's grace, healing, and continued protection," Glenn adds.

They also note that God isn't done yet. The many health challenges and the consequences of those ordeals will never be forgotten. At the same time, the same God who's brought them this far will be with them in everything yet to come.

I've been told that suffering will either make you better or worse as an individual, but one way or the other, you will not come out the other side as the same person you were before. A good friend of mine named Shirley has a saying that sums it up well: "Suffering should make you better, not bitter." This is the code she lives by, and it's a code that I, too, am determined to follow. *Better, not bitter.* It's about allowing the Lord to work through the hard things in life to make you more loving, forgiving, and compassionate instead of hard-hearted, miserable, and angry.

So how have the years of hardship affected Catherine? She told me:

> Those first six years were so scary. Life feels more hopeful and manageable now than it was when Josiah was a baby. I never imagined we'd have four specialist appointments a week when I thought I'd just get to be home with my baby.
>
> Every time you're hit with something new you feel gutted, but you have to come back to God. Josiah is here for a purpose. So many times he could've died, but God has good plans and is sovereign, and we've seen that over and over again. It's not easy, but the easy things in our lives aren't what bring us closer to God. I've come to trust God and to surrender to God—I'm forced to because there's nothing else you can do. You could choose to get angry and bitter, but how's that going to help?
>
> It all seemed unfair at the beginning, but God showed me that He's close to the broken.

Recent testing revealed that one of Josiah's vocal cords is permanently paralyzed, yet he still has a worship voice. Josiah takes singing lessons, writes music, and is a member of a youth worship team. He also plays the drums and piano, but singing is his favorite outlet. Josiah doesn't have the same physical stamina for sports as some other boys his age, but God has gifted him with a voice that proclaims the glory of the Lord—and a heart that beats to praise his Savior.

+ + +

It's only natural, I think, that I, too, wondered about other scenarios. *What if we'd received a diagnosis in which treatment wasn't even an option? What if we knew with certainty that our baby boy would pass away at or shortly after birth? How would we process the situation? How would we prepare for the birth of one healthy baby and one who would die? Could my heart handle the bittersweet joy of pregnancy—both twins born alive, even if only for the moment—knowing that their birthday would also be our baby boy's last, knowing that I would be caring for one healthy newborn while preparing for the funeral of the other?*

I knew we faced that possibility, yet at least our unborn son had a *chance*. But many parents don't even have that hope. They treasure precious moments with their preborn child—talking to him, singing to him, praying for him—savoring the short time they have. Yet as the due date draws near, they prepare to caress a silent baby in their arms, prepare to tend to broken hearts, prepare to say goodbye. Love and grief all at once. What an impossible reality.

Though the preparations and prayers would be different, our source of strength would remain the same. The same verses, the same loving God, the same ultimate hope of reuniting in heaven would comfort us in the pain.

My heart aches for those who find themselves in this agonizing place. If that's you, though our journeys are different, may I encourage you? Hold fast to the Lord with all the strength you can muster, and turn to Jesus, our comforter. He says to you, "Come to Me, all who are weary and burdened, and I will give you rest. Take My yoke upon you and learn from Me, for I am gentle and humble in heart, and you will find rest for your souls. For My yoke is comfortable, and My burden is light" (Matthew 11:28-30, NASB).

Meanwhile, if you have received a life-threatening prenatal diagnosis and are looking for practical support, factual information, and stories of those who have walked a similar path, please consider visiting prenataldiagnosis.org or perinatalhospice.org.

+ + +

Receiving an unfavorable prenatal diagnosis is hard, and losing a child is unimaginable. Thiago and Karynne have endured both situations, and they're united in their advice to those facing either scenario: Decide to trust God.

"Trusting God is a decision, not a feeling," they say. "It's a decision that must be rooted in the Word of God. Don't give in or give up. If He's with us, we can make it, whether the outcome is good or bad."

I resonate with their words. Navigating the tumultuous seas of a life-threatening prenatal diagnosis and the delivery of a critically ill child was just the beginning of the most physically, emotionally, mentally, and spiritually trying time of my life. For four years after Nathaniel's birth, I struggled each day just to keep my head above water—survival was my only goal. They were traumatic years filled with the stress and anxiety of caring for my three young children as well as experiencing a subsequent cancer diagnosis and treatment.

During that same time period I also experienced relational struggles that led to uncertainty and fear, marital issues, and a physically depleted body that gave out on me more than once. If not for the Lord, I would have surely drowned. But God never let go of me. As the Lord helped me dig out from beneath trauma and hurt, I learned to trust in Him like never before.

I've learned to cling to God's Word like a shipwrecked sailor to a life preserver. Remaining in the Word and in prayer has kept me afloat. Many times I've cried out to God in my pain, confusion, despair, and anger. I know He can handle my questions and my lament. If you, too, are seeking His voice, might I suggest that Psalms 42, 86, and 91 are good places to begin. I've also found encouragement in songs of worship; perhaps you will too.

As much as possible, surround yourself with mature believers—trusted loved ones and friends who can support you as you face the tough decisions of life. People who will pray with you and for you and your family; people who will also sit with you in silence when words just aren't enough. I discovered extra insight in *A Lifetime of Wisdom: Embracing the Way God Heals You* by Joni Eareckson Tada, a godly woman who's known decades of suffering—and what it means to cling to Jesus—since she became a quadriplegic after a freak diving accident at age seventeen. Her remarkable story of faith, grit, determination, humility, and strength in the face of unbearable pain and loss has made an indelible impression.

I've learned to cling to God's Word like a shipwrecked sailor to a life preserver.

Finally, let's endeavor to do as Paul exhorts in Philippians 4:8: "Finally, brothers, whatever is true, whatever is honorable, whatever is just, whatever is pure, whatever is lovely, whatever is commendable, if there is any excellence, if there is anything worthy of praise, think about these things."

Joy and peace in the midst of turmoil *are* possible through the working of God's Spirit in us. I know it's easier said than done, but don't give up. Put your strength and hope in Jesus in both the good times and the bad. Because He is good *all* the time.

Epilogue

May the God of hope fill you with all joy and peace in believing, so that by the power of the Holy Spirit you may abound in hope.

ROMANS 15:13

When Nathaniel came home, he fit in like the missing piece of our family puzzle. Thomas simply adored his baby brother now that they were able to be together. I can still recall Nathaniel intently watching Thomas do a loud and exuberant dance for his rapt audience of one—skinny infant Nathaniel, who was laughing hysterically at his big brother's crazy antics. Sometimes I'd set Nathaniel and Emma beside each other on a blanket, and I got a fright more than once when Thomas, my ball of energy, leaped over them before I had a chance to act. (By God's mercy Thomas never landed on them!) *This* was why everyone wanted Nathaniel to come home—home was the place where he'd receive the love and stimulation and joy that could only come from his family.

To our great surprise and relief, by the end of Nathaniel's first week home he was able to finish a whole bottle on his own, so I never had to replace his feeding tube. After his tube was removed he fed normally from that day forward. And by the end of the summer Nathaniel had been taken off all medications.

Our tiny home was full of toys, mats, infant chairs, high chairs, playpens—you name it. Keeping the place neat and tidy was not a priority; keeping the kids fed, changed, content, and loved was. Physical and emotional exhaustion was the regular state of being for Mau and me during those first few months. In some ways it was like our life during Nathaniel's ten-week hospital stay—my parents continued coming by every day to help me and to stay with Thomas and Emma when I had to take Nathaniel to one follow-up appointment or another. I averaged at least one per week for that first year.

As Nathaniel gained weight, his appearance transformed. He showed up in our home as a scrawny, wizened, and bald baby with wrinkles etched into his forehead from all he'd endured. His tongue hung out due to weak facial muscles after being intubated for weeks. By early fall, however, he was a plump and rosy little guy with dark brown hair making its return on his once-shaved head.

Mau's parents came from Brazil to stay for a month. It was a gift for them to spend time with their grandkids after only receiving updates from afar. They were able to join us at church for a special service to dedicate the twins and to publicly thank the Lord for saving Nathaniel. We invited the entire church, family, and friends, plus Nathaniel's nurse Amber.

We welcomed everyone by reading Psalm 95:1-5 and followed that with singing and a slideshow of Nathaniel's journey from hospital to home. After a prayer from my mother, our whole family—grandparents included—made our way to the front, where our pastor dedicated Nathaniel and Emma to the Lord. It was an unforgettable evening.

+ + +

In early August I received a call from a foundation that raises money for research and technology to help treat sick kids.

A woman from the charity explained, "We heard about Nathaniel's extraordinary recovery, and we'd like to feature him in our quarterly publication."

"Really?" I exclaimed. "You're very welcome to feature him. How do we go about doing that?"

"I'll need you to send me some pictures of Nathaniel in the hospital and some pictures of him today, and one of my colleagues will call to interview you and your husband."

I went through the photos I had taken of Nathaniel on my phone. By this time Nathaniel's strength had improved so much that he could lift his head without any difficulty and keep his tongue in his mouth. I sent in the photos, and we did the interview, and a month later we received a big envelope with copies of the publication. Nathaniel's adorable face filled the front cover.

The foundation had also interviewed a doctor from the children's hospital, so we learned more about his situation than was ever explained to us. The article actually explained why so many doctors at the maternity clinic had been reluctant to offer Nathaniel treatment. The surgeons at the children's hospital, thankfully, had a different perspective:

> [Nathaniel] was so sick that he would not have typically been considered a candidate for surgery at other hospitals. However, based on results from their study, Nathaniel's surgeons knew they could help. They challenged the criteria that had been established in the 1990s—criteria

> that would have deemed him inoperable. Given new developments in medicine and in surgery, the team's research showed that the criteria were in need of changes, and that there was an opportunity to save more infants' lives. . . .
>
> So the team gathered the data to show that more aggressive treatment can be effective. Their research findings . . . were so compelling that they are now influencing surgical practice across North America.[1]

After reading the article I felt even more grateful for the surgery team's willingness to operate on Nathaniel—to even give him a chance. I realized that our insistence that the doctors try to save him, and their belief that he could indeed be saved, led not only to Nathaniel's treatment and survival but also to further research and improved surgical practices. It's incredible to think that other babies with severe CDH have survived as a result of Nathaniel's journey! My hope is that couples who receive a prenatal diagnosis of CDH today are met with optimism by their doctors—that they receive hope and not despair.

Our insistence that the doctors try to save him, and their belief that he could indeed be saved, led not only to Nathaniel's treatment and survival but also to further research and improved surgical practices.

It would be easy to attribute Nathaniel's success to advances in medical skill and technology. While I'm certainly no theologian, I believe his survival was a combination of both medical treatment and the work of the Lord. I see the medical advancements that benefited Nathaniel as an example of God's grace. Medical treatment is a gift from God whether one recognizes it that way or not. No doubt Nathaniel was a recipient of this gift, but we also saw the Lord move each step of the way. Against all odds, Nathaniel often did *better than expected*.

When we come up against a seemingly insurmountable obstacle and fear sets in, our vision sometimes becomes myopic. We often fail to see the bigger picture. But when we allow faith to displace fear, that's when our field of vision expands, the impossible becomes possible, and we see God at work. We couldn't yet see the full picture God had in store when we first received Nathaniel's diagnosis. It might take a lifetime before we ever know the extent of God's plans, but it sure is exciting to watch them unfurl.

As I think about our journey I'm reminded of Paul's words about the unseen world. In Ephesians 6:12, he writes, "We do not wrestle against flesh and blood, but against the rulers, against the authorities, against the cosmic powers over this present darkness, against the spiritual forces of evil in the heavenly places." While it seemed like we were merely struggling to convince doctors to help save our son, a spiritual battle was also taking place. This battle, invisible to our human eyes, is a fight for babies who deserve a chance at life as well as a fight for the family members involved.

To fend off spiritual attacks Mau and I had to shield ourselves with our faith. The arrows flew toward us in rapid succession: *Your son will die. The odds are against you. You should have a reduction. He might have other congenital defects. You should have a termination. CDH kids have long-term health issues. You should consider palliation. There are worse things than death. Your son won't make it.*

You should have an abortion. Each arrow aimed to pierce our hope; each arrow tried to convince us to kill our baby.

But the enemy *did not win*. With each arrow we said, "We trust in God. We'll let the Lord decide. We serve a God of *life*. Our God is bigger than any diagnosis. Whether He takes our child to his heavenly home or allows us to take him to his earthly home, God alone rules."

How did we inform our faith and fend off spiritual attacks? We raised our "sword of the Spirit, which is the word of God" (Ephesians 6:17). There is life and power in God's Word. In Scripture the Lord repeatedly exhorts us to "fear not." As it says in Deuteronomy 31:8, "It is the LORD who goes before you. He will be with you; he will not leave you or forsake you. Do not fear or be dismayed." We remained determined in the face of opposition by knowing His Word, remaining in His Word, and returning to His Word.

If you're reading this book and you've received a devastating prenatal diagnosis or simply find yourself pregnant under difficult circumstances, I'd like to speak directly to you: First of all, congratulations on your pregnancy! Children are a precious gift from the Lord, and God knows what He's doing. I implore you not to give in to fear. Rest assured that with the Lord on your side you're in very good hands. He knows what you're going through. He understands your pain and confusion. If you draw near to Him, you'll find that He is faithful and ready to welcome you into His arms.

The Lord says to us in Isaiah 41:10:

Fear not, [*insert your name*,] for I am with you;
  be not dismayed, for I am your God;
I will strengthen you, I will help you,
  I will uphold you with my righteous right hand.

He'll be with you as you make the hard decisions. Cry out to the Lord each step of the way, pray with expectation that He will hear you and make a way, and trust that He indeed sees the big picture.

Isaiah 43:1-3, 19 makes it clear that the Lord loves us and will carry us through whatever difficulties life throws our way:

But now thus says the LORD,
he who created you, O Jacob,
  he who formed you, O Israel:
"Fear not, for I have redeemed you;
  I have called you by name, you are mine.
When you pass through the waters, I will be with you;
  and through the rivers, they shall not overwhelm you;
when you walk through fire you shall not be burned,
  and the flame shall not consume you.
For I am the LORD your God,
  the Holy One of Israel, your Savior. . . .

"Behold, I am doing a new thing;
  now it springs forth, do you not perceive it?
I will make a way in the wilderness
  and rivers in the desert."

Choosing the path of faith, of life—the path that at first glance often seems more difficult—isn't a guarantee that things will turn out the way we want. The Lord promises us in this passage that He will be *with us* as we go through the waters, rivers, and fire, not that we won't encounter them at all. Mau and I passed through the waters, but we didn't drown. We passed through the fire (and definitely felt the heat!), but we didn't burn. Was our journey easy? Not at all. Do I regret choosing life for Nathaniel? Not for a second. I know that that's easier for me to say because our son survived, but I like to believe that I would do it all over again, ten times out of ten, even if it ended differently. Of course it was hard, but it was worth it.

Above all, we didn't need or want to play God. We leave life-and-death decisions about our children in His hands. We give God the opportunity to do His will as He pleases. There is an inexplicable peace that comes from leaving that burden on His capable shoulders. We knew that choosing abortion for our child would not bring us peace. It would not give us closure. How my heart aches for every mother or father haunted by the ghosts of trauma, grief, and depression brought on by abortion. In the same way, my heart is filled with compassion for every parent who mourns the broken dream of giving birth to a healthy child or who faces a crisis pregnancy. God sees you in your suffering. "The LORD is near to the brokenhearted and saves the crushed in spirit" (Psalm 34:18).

Choosing the path of faith, of life—the path that at first glance often seems more difficult—isn't a guarantee that things will turn out the way we want.

And what of Canada? Is there any hope for this country that places so little value on human life? Has God given up on us? I'm convinced that He hasn't.

A few years ago I joined with a group of like-minded people from across the country who pray to see the end of abortion in Canada. I no longer feel alone in my convictions. Together we pray that abortion-minded women (and men) will find hope and courage in Christ to choose life for their children. We pray for hearts to heal from past abortions and for the Canadian healthcare culture to change. We pray that spiritually blind eyes will open and hard hearts will soften. Through this group of believers I have met many who are engaged in the courageous work of "speak[ing] up for those who cannot speak for themselves, for the rights of all who are destitute" (Proverbs 31:8, NIV).

There is an undercurrent of change in Canada. It's not widespread yet, but I believe the Lord is at work. While Canadian women who've had abortions rarely express regret, support for the practice is decreasing among younger Canadians, plus there is a marked decline in the number of Canadian women seeking abortions.[2] Pastors are beginning to talk about this issue in their churches, and some believers have taken action—praying, starting abortion-recovery programs, volunteering with pro-life organizations, engaging politically, and learning how to share their convictions in a winsome way. Yet more voices are needed.

As for my American friends, you have the freedom to speak more openly. Might I encourage you to get involved if you haven't already? There are many ways to make a difference if you're willing to break the silence. May we be motivated by our love and compassion for both mother and child. (For more ideas, visit lovelife.org, an organization committed to partnering with churches across North America, including Canada, to see abortion end.)

If you have a heart for Canada, consider praying with us in the Life Room (liferoom.ca) as we ask the Lord to restore a culture of life in our land.

+ + +

Nothing makes my heart sing more than when I watch my kids enjoying each other's company. Though Thomas is older and the three of them sometimes struggle to find an activity they all enjoy, I often see them playing what we call "Twins." Emma takes the role of Mom while the two boys play the role of twins. If I hear someone call out to "Mom," they're usually not looking for me. (I'm still "Mommy" or "Mama" to them.)

Sometimes the kids and I look at pictures of Nate as a baby in the hospital. (In the months following Nathaniel's release from the hospital, as his physical appearance transformed from gaunt to robust, he transitioned in name from Nathaniel to Nate. The transition was just as gradual as his transition from frailty to strength, from sickness to health.) And when we look at those pictures, as I reminisce about those days and retell the story of how God saved Nate, Thomas pulls his brother into a big bear hug, eyes glistening with tears, and says, "I love you, buddy!"

Moments like these make my soul rejoice. We're certainly not a perfect family, but we love each other a lot. It's hard to imagine our life without Nate in it.

When I tell people who aren't familiar with our story that Nate wasn't expected to live and had to fight hard to survive, they find it hard to believe that he was ever that sick. That little boy who's so full of energy? That boy who loves to run and climb and jump and play just like the other kids his age? That boy with the contagious laugh and the mischievous glint in his eye? That boy who's both rough-and-tumble and sensitive and sweet?

Yes, *that* boy.

Nate's story isn't over. God has much in store for him, and only time will tell how it unfolds. But one thing is certain: Though the early days of Nate's life were fraught with trials, the Lord never left us. I will never forget to say, *Thank You, Lord, for saving Nate.*

Thirty-six weeks pregnant with twins.

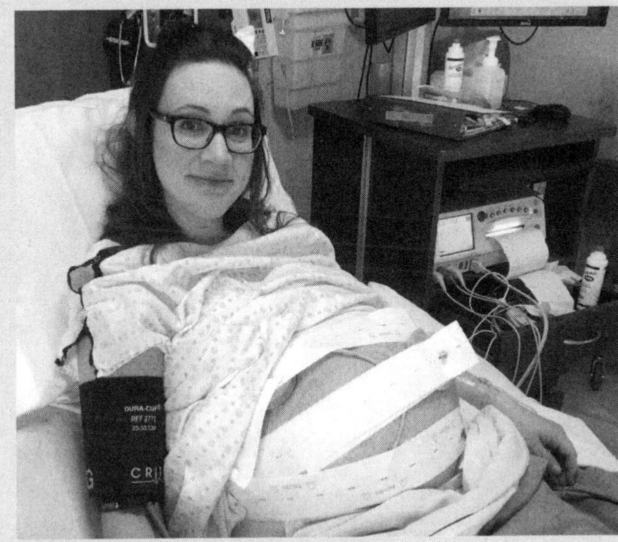

Delivery Day: March 20, 2017

Photo Gallery

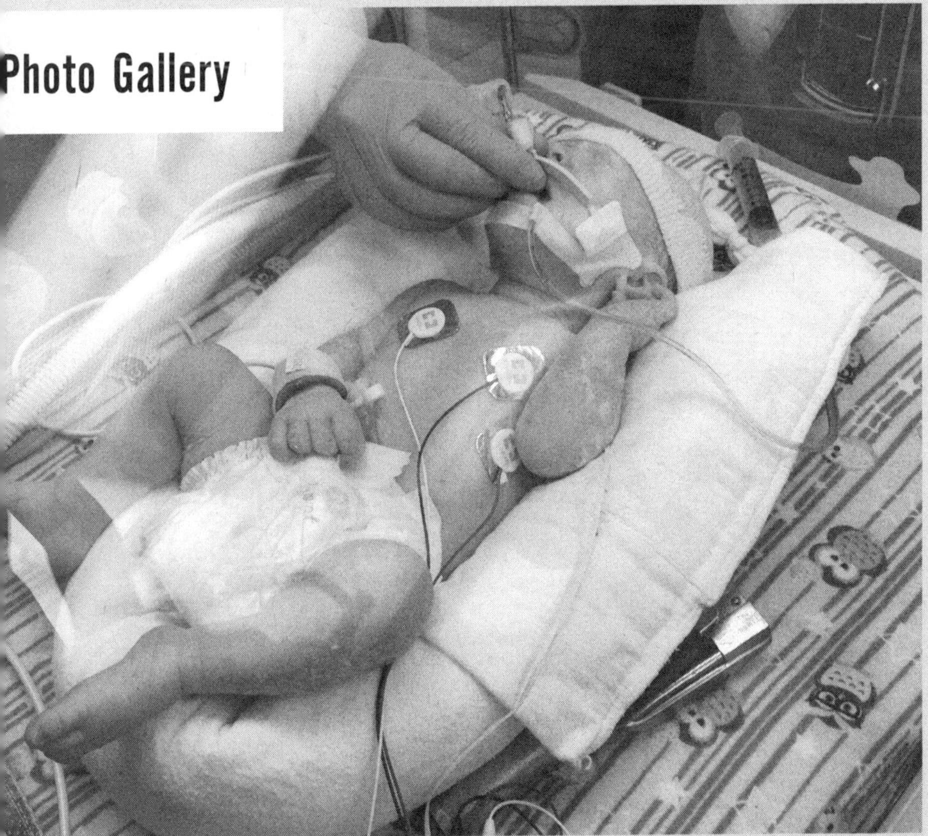

Welcome to the world, Nathaniel!

RIGHT: Mauricio holds Emma in her new handcrafted blanket.

BOTTOM LEFT: Eight-week-old Nathaniel will need supplemental oxygen for a few more days.

BOTTOM RIGHT: Feeding my little boy in the hospital.

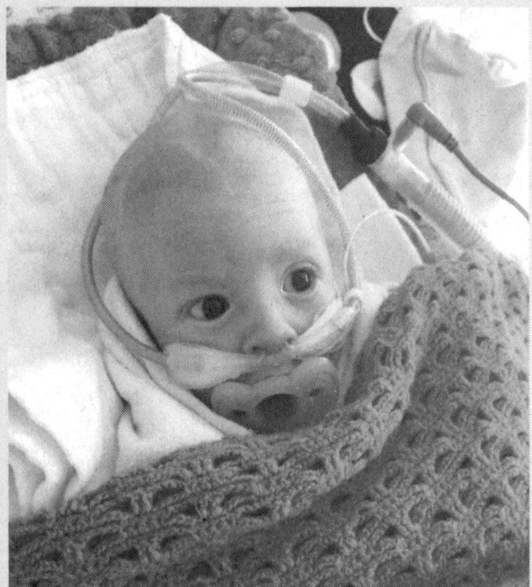

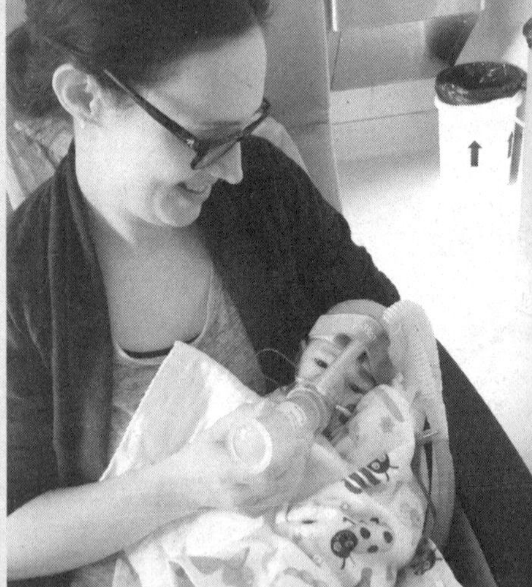

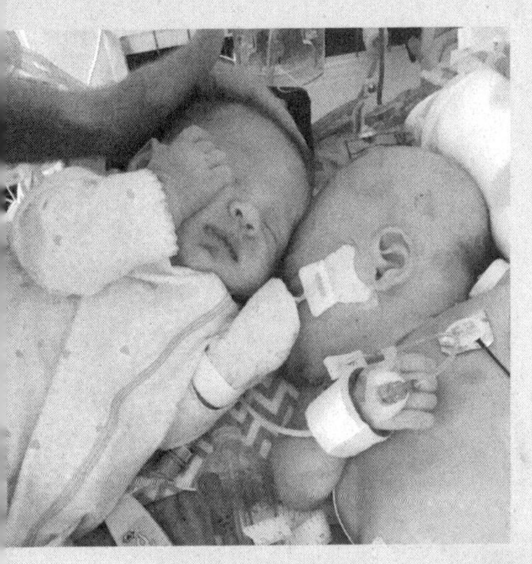

Our twins are reunited!

"[The nurse] suggests we lay Emma beside Nathaniel in his bed for a little while as she sleeps. It will be the first time they've been near each other since sharing my womb. . . . Next thing I know, there they are together—a rosy little girl dressed in a sleeper with pink hearts and a frail little boy dressed in nothing but a diaper over dull skin. My twins are reunited."

After ten weeks in the hospital, we're finally ready to go home.

Our first portrait as a family of five (summer 2017).

Nathaniel at five months old.

The toddler twins in their double stroller.

Now just "Nate"—our budding musician at two years old.

icking berries as a family.

First Day of School 2023: Thomas, Emma, and Nate

This bike park is awesome!" say Emma and Nate.

Me and my seven-year-old survivor.

Our family today.

Notes

CHAPTER 2 | FROM INFERTILITY TO DOUBLE BLESSING

1. Emmanuel Spaggiari et al., "Impact of Including or Removing Nuchal Translucency Measurement on the Detection and False-Positive Rates of First-Trimester Down Syndrome Screening," *Fetal Diagnosis and Therapy* 40, no. 3 (2016): 214–18, December 12, 2015, https://doi.org/10.1159/000442198.
2. Bridget Balch, "Prenatal Screenings Can Lead to False Positives, Heightened Anxiety," Association of American Medical Colleges, April 14, 2022, https://www.aamc.org/news/prenatal-screenings-can-lead-false-positives-heightened-anxiety.
3. "Abortion in Canada," Government of Canada, accessed October 19, 2024, https://www.canada.ca/en/public-health/services/sexual-health/abortion-canada.html.
4. Linda Long, "Abortion in Canada," The Canadian Encyclopedia, updated March 7, 2005, https://www.thecanadianencyclopedia.ca/en/article/abortion.
5. "Abortion Facts: Did You Know?" The Wilberforce Project, accessed May 3, 2024, https://www.thewilberforceproject.ca/about_abortion.

CHAPTER 3 | SHATTERED HOPE

1. "Congenital Diaphragmatic Hernia (CDH)," Children's Hospital of Philadelphia, accessed May 4, 2024, https://www.chop.edu/conditions-diseases/congenital-diaphragmatic-hernia-cdh#.
2. "4.2 Slavery and Abolition in the 19th Century," *Brazil: Five Centuries of Change*, Brown University Library, accessed October 8, 2024, https://library.brown.edu/create/fivecenturiesofchange/chapters/chapter-3/slavery-and-aboliton.

3. "Safe Access Zone Laws and Court Injunctions in Canada (to Protect Abortion Access)," Abortion Rights Coalition of Canada, updated June 12, 2024, https://www.arcc-cdac.ca/media/2020/06/Bubble-Zones-Court-Injunctions-in-Canada.pdf.
4. "Abortion: Brazil," Human Rights Watch, accessed November 5, 2024, https://www.hrw.org/legacy/women/abortion/brazil.html.
5. "Abortion: Brazil."
6. "IBGE: Brazil's Population Reaches 212.6 Million," gov.br, updated September 2, 2024, https://www.gov.br/secom/en/latest-news/2024/08/ibge-brazils-population-reaches-212-6-million.
7. Selena Simmons-Duffin, "Despite Bans in Some States, More than a Million Abortions Were Provided in 2023," NPR, March 19, 2024, https://www.npr.org/sections/health-shots/2024/03/19/1238293143/abortion-data-how-many-us-2023.
8. "U.S. Population 1950–2025," Macrotrends, accessed April 3, 2025, https://www.macrotrends.net/global-metrics/countries/USA/united-states/population.

CHAPTER 5 | A QUEST TO KNOW WHY

1. "Impact on Parents," PrenatalDiagnosis.org, accessed April 30, 2024, https://prenataldiagnosis.org/essentials/family-impact/impact-parents.
2. Laura Huene, interview with the author, November 2024.

CHAPTER 6 | WORDS AND NAMES HAVE MEANING

1. Asaph Rolnitsky et al., "Cost of Neonatal Intensive Care for Extremely Preterm Infants in Canada," *Translational Pediatrics* 10, no. 6 (2021): 1630–36, https://doi.org/10.21037/tp-21-36.
2. "Frequently Asked Questions," Perinatal Hospice and Palliative Care, accessed April 30, 2024, https://www.perinatalhospice.org/faqs.
3. "Birth Planning," Perinatal Hospice and Palliative Care, accessed November 12, 2024, https://www.perinatalhospice.org/birth-planning. Adapted from Amy Kuebelbeck and Deborah L. Davis, *A Gift of Time: Continuing Your Pregnancy When Your Baby's Life Is Expected to Be Brief*, 2nd ed. (Baltimore: Johns Hopkins University Press, 2023).
4. Nancy DeMoss Wolgemuth, Dannah Gresh, and Angie Smith, hosts, *Revive Our Hearts*, podcast, season "I Will Carry You," episode 1, "Band-Aids on a Heart," produced by Revive Our Hearts Ministries, May 24, 2022, https://www.reviveourhearts.com/podcast/revive-our-hearts/band-aids-heart.

CHAPTER 10 | FEAR REARS ITS UGLY HEAD

1. Emily Perl Kingsley, "Welcome to Holland," 1987, https://www.emilyperlkingsley.com/welcome-to-holland.

CHAPTER 13 | BACK TO SQUARE ONE

1. William Goldman, *The Princess Bride* (New York: Random House, 1973).

CHAPTER 17 | THIAGO AND KARYNNE'S STORY

1. Timothy Keller, *Walking with God through Pain and Suffering* (New York: Penguin, 2013), 115.

EPILOGUE

1. "Life-Saving Research for Babies," *Just 4 Kids*, Alberta's Children's Hospital Foundation, Fall 2017, 1–3.
2. Tristin Hopper, "As Many as One in Five Canadian Pregnancies End in Abortion and Few Regret Decision, Poll Finds," *National Post*, November 24, 2022, https://nationalpost.com/news/canada/abortion-in-canada.